Bangladesh Since 1952 Language Movement

Bangladesh Since 1952 Language Movement

Abanti Adhikari

Maulana Abul Kalam Azad Institute of Asian Studies, Kolkata

SHIPRA

ISBN: 978-81-7541-597-3

First Published in India in 2011

Bangladesh Since 1952 Language Movement

Published by:
SHIPRA PUBLICATIONS
H.O.: LG 18-19, Pankaj Central Market, Patparganj,
Delhi-110092, Tel: 91-11-2223 5152, 2223 6152
Br.Off.: 4617/18, Ansari Road, Darya Ganj,
New Delhi-110002, Tel: 6594 6453, 9810522367
E-mail: info@shiprapublications.com
www.shiprapublications.com

Acknowledgements

I am extremely grateful to my teachers, Professor Hari Shankar Vasudevan, Director, Maulana Abul Kalam Azad Institute of Asian Studies and my teacher Professor Tapati Guha-Thakurta of the Centre for Studies in Social Sciences, for their support. I am grateful to Professor Barun De, Dr. Jayanta Kumar Ray, Prof. Mahabir Singh and Dr. Chittabrata Palit also for their guidance and motivation.

I am grateful to Professor Nazur Islam, former UGC Chairperson of Dhaka University, and his family members, including Mansurat Ayesha Nusrat, for their academic guidance. I thank Prof. Ratanlal Chakrobarty and Prof. Meghna Guha Thakurta, former Professors of Dhaka University, Professor Khan Mohammed Mohsin and Delwar Hossain for their support and cooperation.

I also extend my thanks to Dr. Prashanto Mahato, Principal and colleagues, at Narasinha Dutta College, for their guidance during this tedious journey. I thank one of my friends, Mrs. Sudarshana Chowdhury, for her constant inspiration and encouragement.

My regards to my mother Mrs. Chitra Adhikari, former head of the Department of History in a Calcutta College, for her profound help and inspiration. I am grateful to Shipra Publications for its efforts in the correction of mistakes in the manuscript.

Contents

1

Introduction

Religion and the Rise of Capitalism, by R.H. Tawney, a classic study of the development of religious thought in relation to social and economic questions, is one of the major contributions to modern social theory. But the book is even more pertinent now than when it first appeared. For today it is even clearer that the dividing line between the spheres of religion and secular business is shifting.

The object of the book is to trace some strands in the development of religious thought on social and economic questions in the period, in relation to Bangladesh which saw the transition from medieval to modern theories of social organization. It does not carry the subject beyond the beginning of the eighteenth century, and it makes no pretense of dealing with the history either of economic theory or of practice, except in so far as these were related to changes in religious opinion.

The revolutions, at once religious, political and social, which herald the transition from the medieval to the modern world, were hardly less decisive for the economic character of the new civilization than for its ecclesiastical organizations and religious doctrines. It is important to note the development of economic thought in medieval Italy; the social forces at work in the Germany of Luther; and his attitude to them; the economic doctrines of Calvin; the teaching of the Jesuits on usury and allied topics; and the religious and social outlook of the French bourgeoisie of the same period.

Religion: Universal

Religion is as old as history, or even prehistory, and has taken innumerable forms in the past: Judaism, Christianity, Islam, Hinduism,

Buddhism, Chinese and Japanese traditions are some of the oldest religious precepts which have millions of followers. One criterion for selecting these seven traditions is their number of followers. Christianity, Islam and Hinduism easily qualify. The number of Buddhists is more difficult to estimate, but this religion is embraced by a majority of south-east Asians, and is a primary element of Japanese and Chinese traditions. Precisely how many Chinese—especially among the 1.2 billion citizens of the People's Republic—continue to adhere to religious practices is hard to judge, but even a conservative estimate would go to reach hundreds of millions. Christianity and Islam would cover at least a major part of the world population. However, as modern scholars have noted, 'any definition of religion has to be arbitrary to a certain extent', and whatever is narrated, as definition of religion would cover, either 'too much' or 'too little' or both. In a very simple form, religion may be said to include the 'history of Gods, men and the universe', and in a roughly erected framework, may be termed as a 'collection of statements about God, Providence, immortality, and myths and rituals[1] Kolkakowski declares, he considers the 'act of worship as unremovable and intrinsic to any description of the phenomenon of religion'.

Historically, Christianity and Islam in particular have been active missionary religions, spreading far beyond their places of origin. In the modern world, Muslim, Hindu and Chinese migrants have taken their religious beliefs and practices to most areas of the world. Likewise, Buddhism, born in India, has spread widely from its original heartland in China, and has profoundly affected the religious lives of Asians, and, in more recent times, of many Westerners.

World Religions: The Illustrious Guide, seeks to convey, among other things, the compelling mysteries, the profound intellectual aspects and the depth of faith that the world's major religions have achieved: how they have helped to shape the general landscape of cultures and provided traditions of prayer, meditation and healing, and rituals that lend much meaning to life.

Today, in some quarters, the old certainties of different religions are being challenged by modernizing influences and scholarly discoveries; elsewhere, a new religious radicalism is being fostered. In fact, the religious situation in much of the world has become increasingly complex. The coexistence of many religious traditions of different geographic origins have made individuals more curious about the religious tradition of their neighbours, and groups, and scholars are devoting more attention to the study and understanding of their cultures other than their own.

Clarifying these complex issues in a thoroughly accessible text, *World Religions: The Illustrious Guide* gives a penetrating introduction to the extraordinary diversity of the world's great faiths as also their profoundly fascinating common concerns. Focussing on the seven most important religions in terms of numbers of adherents, historical significance and diffusion, the book brings depth and clarity to the major themes of these traditions through a wealth of reference information, including maps and charts.

All belief systems are intimately bound up with the development of the cultures from which they have emerged, the roots of which often lie in distant prehistory. The sources that describe the origins of a faith may date from a much later period than the events that they describe, and frequently they incorporate mythological and historical accounts.

All religious traditions acknowledge certain times of the day, the year, the human life cycle, and even history as times of special proximity to the sacred occasions to be marked by private or communal acts of religious observance. The cosmic rhythms of the sun, moon, planets, and stars are noted and marked in the religious calendar; dawn and sunset are widely considered times of particular holiness. The world's major religious traditions have both reflected and shaped the values of the societies of which they have been an inseparable element. Historically, religious leaders have been influential in setting national, moral, social and political agendas, and this remains true in many countries today. However, the rise of modern secular government has sometimes created tensions between the civil and religious establishments. But many of the issues that face present-day societies raise ethical questions that go to the heart of central, often longstanding, religious concerns.

Religion, for the societies and peoples in Asia and Africa, commonly encapsulates people's values and ideas, sets forward their role models and is integrally related to a sense of identity for many. The study of religion is therefore concerned with the inspiration (for good/ill) of people's culture, history and beliefs connecting ultimate issues. It is impossible to understand any culture without studying its religion, which is defined as, how people reflect on and react to what they consider to be the basis of their existence.

Important aspects of some religions are a form of extreme conservatism, marked as 'fundamentalism', which is now seen in many countries of the world. The essence of religious fundamentalism is extremely hard to define, and may be roughly regarded as a charismatic attitude regarding the superiority of one's own religion. This aggressive religious devotion to a certain religion is often creating a deep intolerance towards other religions, making confusion and imbalance in the world religious order.

Fundamentalism in Bangladesh between 1971 and 2004 is mainly a study of religious-cum-superstitious tendencies in the country after independence of Bangladesh. The question is, how far they could gain a foothold in the next twenty-five years, before the rise of the Awami League government. Here of course, 'fundamentalism' stands only for Islamic fundamentalism, since the Hindus, Christians and Buddhists form the religious minorities in the country, but the discussion leaves out fundamentalist aspects of the minority religious tenets. As will be seen, 'fundamentalism' has a religious connotation also.

Religion and Politics

There has always been a close connection between religion and politics, even in the very remote past. Religious issues had been brought forward in the west, such as in classical Greece and Rome. Socrates had been punished and given death penalty, because it was said, he was training the youth of Greece to be non-conformists, with regard to the current faith. In imperial Rome, thousands of Christians were killed due to the caprices of the emperor, because they were embracing Christianity. The medieval European history is a long tale of confrontation and conciliation between the German emperor and the Papacy. In ancient Asia, Buddhism had been patronized by Emperor Asoka and thrown around the neighbouring countries, so that, thousands of Buddhists are still living in China and other parts of East Asia. Emperors Akbar the Great in Mughal India, and later Napoleon Bonaparte in Europe, had used religion to strengthen their own political power. In this way, innumerable examples can be picked up from the past history to indicate the positive relationship between religion and politics in different parts of the world at distinct times.

The nexus between religion and politics provides an important focus for studies of comparative politics. First, certain religious traditions may provide a cross-cultural identity and identification, which may well facilitate the task of important political analysis. Therefore, the role of the Church in resisting democratization in Spain and in some parts of South America, as also the resistance of East European countries to a Communist regime after 1945, because of its anti-Christian character, would provide examples of cooperation and conflict between politics and religion.

Similarly, the wide scope of Islam makes it possible to compare the role of religion in politics between countries in which Muslims constitute a large majority of citizens (Iran, Algeria), with areas in which Muslims are a consequential political minority (India, Western Europe). Examining the emergence of Bangladesh in the later part of twentieth century, the significant question is that, what role religion plays in countries where Islam is the basis of political organization, and in other nations such as Russia, that had witnessed the traces of a communist culture.

Similarly, in Iran, Islamic activists led a powerful revolution in 1979, when religious leaders then outmaneuvered their secular allies and established an Islamic state headed by the Ayatollah Khomeini, overthrowing the regime headed by the Shah. Today Iran debates limits on the power of religious authorities, while at the same time activists in other countries seek to copy Iranian revolution, or to pressurise their government to pass laws more in accordance with the Koran.

In Western Europe levels of public religiosity had declined to low levels, and predictions that secularism would soon sweep the United States and the rest of the world were common place; by the end of the millennium religion was expected to be confined primarily to less developed societies, and government and politics were expected to be freed of religious bindings. In Lutheran Sweden, Catholics are free to practice their religion, and establish Catholic schools and charities.

The study of Indo-U.S. relations over the years has indeed assumed a plural and spectroscopic character. The relations have been analysed from a variety of perspectives, viz., political, security, economic, social and cultural. Gita Roy in her book, *The Duel of the Decade*, seeks to bring into bold relief the political and security aspects of the relations between these two nations, India and the U.S.A., vis-à-vis Pakistan and China over a limited period between 1962 and 1972.

Fifty years ago, many social scientists assumed that "religion in the modern world was declining and would likely to continue to decline until its eventual disappearance".[2] In Western Europe levels of public religiosity had declined to low levels, and many assumed this to be the likely path of most societies. Predictions that secularism would soon sweep the United States and the rest of the world were common place. By the end of the millennium religion was expected to be confined primarily to less developed societies. At the very least, governments and politics were expected to be freed of the influence of religious elites and citizens. However, the example of creation of Pakistan in 1947 as an Islamic state, and the Iranian Revolution of 1979 as a profound fundamentalist structure do not fit in with such ideas and predictions.

Samuel Huntington argues, it has been quoted, "In the modern world, religion is a central, perhaps the central, force that motivates and mobilizes people".[3] Huntington sees a religious revival underway at the end of the twentieth century. This means that religion is today a source of political mobilzation in many nations, and also the source of policy disputes over the relationship between church and state.

In many nations across the world, religion is the source of important political conflicts. Clearly the revitalization of religious tradition crosses international boundaries, and creates currents of world politics. Across the globe, many Islamic adherents are demanding that their government and laws adhere to religious teachings, and many national and local movements drew their inspiration from the successes of Islamic activities in Iran. Regimes in diverse countries like Morocco, Jordan, Indonesia, Algeria and Bangladesh have responded in different ways to this pressure.

In Korea and in Latin America, these religious changes have become interwined with politics, with the new religious traditions providing support, infrastructure, and resources for certain political forces. Baptists are making inroads in Russia, and have provoked a reaction among the Orthodox leadership.

Democratic, authoritarian, totalitarian and *sultanistic* regimes may establish quite different relationships with dominant and minority religious traditions. They differ in the nature and type of authority and legitimacy, the degree of elite and mass pluralism, in their control of important resources, such as media and military, and in countless other dimensions. All these can affect the relationship between the regime and religious groups, bring about different problems at distinct levels of the society and the state—among the poor and the rich, the half-educated and the superior intelligentsia.

Political instability is a persistent feature in many parts of the Muslim world, since political elites in most of the Muslim countries have failed to establish strong and stable institutions. In consequence, Islam has become politically important for the elites, to keep themselves in power. The military-bureaucratic regimes, and the authoritarian kings and sheikhs who are mostly at the helm of affairs in these countries, found it convenient to have persistently used the religion to establish their legacy and embodiment of power. There also has been a persistent tendency to brand Islam as militant, puritanical and violent inspiration.

The doctrinaires of Islamic fundamentalism project a polity where social justice prevails, as prescribed by the Islamic '*Shariah*', which involve both political and economic justice. According to Syed Anwar Hosain, the familiar slogans often heard of in Bangladesh in support of the Islamic system have great resemblance to the socialistic system of the same kind.[4] The one notable example of this type is, '*Anno, Bastro, Basasthan: Islam Debe Samadhan*'.[5] The Muslim countries, like Bangladesh, where gross maldistribution of wealth exists side by side with a growing class-consciousness among certain sections of the population, the ordinary people are particularly vulnerable to militant Islamic propaganda. The Revolution in Iran is an example of Islamic proleterianism that is likely to be repeated elsewhere. So, contrary to the expectation that religion might become a matter of little importance in the technologically advanced world of our times, it is apparent that, "in 2000, religion is resurgent".[6]

Religion has actually become one of the most important political mobilizations of our times. As has already been mentioned, Islamic activists made a successful coup by bringing Ayatollah Khomeini in power and in India, during 1990-02, "the saffron-robe agitators", created a Hindu revivalist tradition which was really anti-secular. The USA also proved to be no expectation. The 2000 Presidential election witnessed considerable political mobilization in spite of that country being known as the epitome of democracy and religious toleration. It is pointed out by scholars that, both George Bush and the opposition Presidential nominee Al Gore seriously talked of Christian doctrines and practices, to tab the minds of religious voters. In this way, all over the world, in south America/Israel, religion has continued to create tension and influence politics. It may be mentioned that, Christian missionaries from Europe and United States continued to spread their traditions abroad, and winning converts from Buddhism, as in south Korea. Such religious trends definitely have their repercussions on any given political situation, pulling and pushing parties with their resources and abilities. To say the least, the search in Hindu nationalism, although confined to India, has definitely created tension between Pakistan and Bangladesh.

Religion and Politics in Different Nation-States (Organisation of Islamic Countries)

Priestly religions may enhance or legitimate political authority in a variety of ways. National or sub-national regimes may support particular religions in a variety of ways. At one extreme, governments may establish official national religions, such as Islam in Iran, Catholicism in Spain and Ireland, Lutheranism in Sweden, or Anglicism in England.

There are important consequences when religion becomes a part of regime and national identity. First, a commitment to a shared set of religious symbols or doctrines may be an extremely political resource in times of political upheaval.

Religious identity is more often a potent source of change than of stability. The cases of Poland, Iran and India suggest that religiously based regimes are subject to competition from both religious and secular sources of opposition.

Religion may serve as an essentially private resource for political and social criticism. In a cultural setting characterized by high levels of religious diversity, it may be difficult for the faithful to attract sufficient support for religious or moral judgements to engage in efficacious political participation.

The Organisation of Islamic Countries (OIC) is a political-cum-religious organization that meets sometimes as a diplomatic forum, and enters into diplomatic negotiations amongst themselves. Bangladesh is a part of this organization, and the respective Prime Ministers of Bangladesh enters into diplomatic negotiations with the different leaders of OIC. This forum is lead mostly by different oil-producing nations of the middle-east, who determine oil prices in the world market. The Organisation of Islamic countries, as a definite religious forum, draws resolutions condemning the spread of Islamic terrorism in different regions of Asia and other areas in the world. It keeps connection with the capitalist nation of the world, and has many subsidiary organizations with it, such as OPEC (Oil and Patrol Exporting Countries), that have a monopolistic control on oil products in the Gulf area. The OIC functions as a political forum and accepts democratic order and social stability as its principles.

Bangladesh, although it is not oil-producing country, is a member of the OIC. The leaders of the nation-state attend the conferences of the OIC that generally take place in any one of the countries of the middle-east. Although there was a pledge for secularism in any one of the constitutions of Bangladesh, still the leaders keep unity and solidarity with the theocratic countries.

Notes

1. Leszek Kolakowski, Religion p. 12.
2. Ted Gerard Jelen and Clyde Wilcox edited, *Religion and Politics in Comparative Perspective*, p. 1.
3. *Ibid.*, p. 1.
4. Syed Anwar Hosain, 'Islamic Fundamentalism in Bangladesh: Internal Variables and External Inputs' in Rafiuddin Ahmed edited, *Religion, Nationalism and Politics in Bangladesh* (South Asian Publishers, New Delhi) p. 145.
5. *Ibid.*, p. 144.
6. *Religion and Politics*, chapter 1, p. 1.

2

Muslim Community in Bangladesh

There has been a host of literature on the study of the Indian Muslims as a community and their aspirations for gaining political leadership in the twentieth century. Historians like Rafiuddin Ahmed and a few others have tried to analyse the identity of this group—who were successful in the partition of India on grounds of religion and the creation of the state of Pakistan, with its two wings.

According to Asim Roy's scholarly account, *The Islamic Syncretistic Tradition in Bengal*, the *pir*s, by combining the dual role of spiritual guides and pioneering leaders of new settlements, contributed very substantially to the peaceful conversion of the lower and poorer classes in Bengal to Islam. Although Islam was a dynamic religion with an egalitarian ideal, its expansion in Bengal neither produced social equality nor promoted the spirit of individual freedom. Muslims in Bengal were polarised very early into two classes. The immigrants from outside and those who claimed to be their descendants constituted the small elite group of *ashraf*s: they sought to maintain their ethnic-cultural separateness and superiority by prescribing rules of endogamy and cultivating Arabic and Persian languages. They thus formed the highest caste among the Muslims as did the *brahmana*s among the Hindus.[1] The majority of the Bengali Muslims who were converts from the lower classes formed the *ajlf*s (corrupted in Bengali into the word *atrap*).

The Muslims made their in-roads in Bengal apparently in the late medieval period. In Bengal the onslaught of Islam had a mixed result on the Bengalee community. On one side, the Hindu high castes in the late Sultanate age collaborated with the alien rulers thus gaining material rewards of collaboration, and at the same time their caste rules and taboos increasingly became more stringent and elaborate, to retain their traditional social privileges and caste identity. On the other side, there was a religious and social movement to make Hinduism more egalitarian by emphasizing *bhakti marga* of the Hindu tradition. There is still another point to note in the context of social formation of Muslims. In spite of their deep loyalty of all these seats to Faith, Bengali Muslim cultivators were tolerant of Hindu practices. They even participated here and there in Hindu religious ceremonies and festivals (e.g. the famous *Janmastomi* procession of Dhaka).

The Bengali authors look on the division of the Bengali Muslim population in another way. Chandi Prasad Sarkar's book, *The Bengali Muslims*: *A Study in their Politicization (1912-1919*) published in 1991, makes a distinction between the Bengali Muslims and the Muslims in Bengal. These two are not identical categories. Whereas the Muslims in Bengal necessarily include a sizeable number of Urdu-speaking non-Bengali Muslims, residing mainly in metropolitan, industrial and urban areas, the Bengali Muslims, besides being the overwhelmingly majority of their community and permanent residents of the province, speak Bengali as their mother-tongue. This distinction has an important bearing on the study of the Bengali Muslims. Islam in medieval Bengal was the religion of the conquerors but not of the conquered, nor effectively of the new converts. Together with an exotic Islamic culture of the immigrants, a parallel folk-culture originating in and covering the various aspects of the Bengali rural life continued to flourish and transform the Islamic identity of the local converts. Consequently there arose a typically Bengali form of Islam not quite conforming to the orthodox canonical principles.

The features of the Bengali Muslim society can be enumerated in the following pattern. Bengali Muslims were accused of communalism also for their persistent refusal to be swallowed up by Hindu religion and culture. Curiously enough, idolatry survived in some form or other among the Bengali Muslims who also continued to be affected by the caste-system in their social life and behavioural pattern.

In the first place, unlike the Hindu practice of disallowing low castes from directly performing certain rites and rituals, the Bengali Muslims of all ethnic groups could generally enter the mosques and participate in the congregational prayers and even get their children admitted to *maktab*s without restriction. This was clearly an egalitarian aspect of the Muslim society in contrast to the Hindus.

Secondly, as among the Hindus, quite a variety of religious sects, sub sects and socio-religious formations characterized the Bengali Muslim society. Divided as the Sunnis were into *Hanafi*, *Shafi*, *Maliki and Hambali* in their religious observances, they agreed to hold the *Shias* in contempt. Again, apart from these two religious sects, there were the *Muhammadia*s or the followers of Muhammad, the Prophet, mainly in north Bengal, with their own mosques in '*Lalbagh*' and *Phulerhat* and a *madrasseh* at Parbatipur. According to the Census Report of 1911, out of the total Muslim population of about twenty four million in Bengal, more than twenty million and a half depended for livelihood on cultivation directly or indirectly.[2] From the Report of the Hornell Committee (1916) it appears that for every twenty-two male Hindu literates, there were only nine male Muslim literates and that against thirty-seven male Hindu literates in English, there were only six such male Muslims.[3] In 1911, only 4 per cent of the total Muslim population were educated; of them 0.25 per cent were English educated.

Meanwhile, towards the last quarter of the nineteenth century some traditionally educated Bengali Muslims—*Munshis*, *Maulavis*, *Mollah*s etc.—who feared that the Christian and Brahmo missionary activities might spread among Muslims, launched a movement to protect their religion and culture from the alien cultural onslaught.

Lack of adequate evidence makes it difficult to place the protagonists of the Mass Contacts campaign in relation to their social, occupational and political backgrounds. A rough survey, however, indicates that they were mostly urban based and drawn largely from professional classes: lawyers, students and teachers sharing socialist and Marxist ideas; journalists such as Syed Ali Ahmad, editor of a leading Patna-based weekly *Itehad*; Syed Abdullah Brevli and Mohammed Nazir, editors of the *Bombay Chronicle* and *Mussawir*, respectively; Maulana Mujibur Rahman, founder and editor of the leading Calcutta newspaper *Mussalman*; Hayatullah Ansari, editor of the *Hindustan Weekly*, published first from Lucknow and later from Delhi; and Mohammad Ismail and Mohammed Jafri, editors of the Delhi newspapers *Daily Qaumi Akhbar* and *Millat*. Some sections of the mass contact leadership had been associated with Congress from the Khilafat days and were connected with the All-India Nationalist Muslim Party and the Congress Muslim party, organizations founded in early 1929 to canvas support for the Nehru Report; others were drawn into the organization during the 1930-2 Civil Disobedience movement.[4]

The Jamiyat-al-ulama was founded in the wake of the Khilafat agitation in December 1919 and its alliance was with Congress, although under strain in the aftermath of the non-co-operation movement, remained largely intact. The Jamiyat, in the next decade, had leaders like Husain Ali Madani, Ahmad Said, Ataullah Shah Bukhari, Hifzur Rehman and others with Congress continued uninterruptedly. In June 1937 a number of this group worked for the Congress candidate in the crucial Bundelkhand election and toured various parts of United Provinces (UP) in connection with the Mass Contacts campaign.

In August 1937 Husain Ahmad Madani, president of Jamiyat-al-Ulema, appealed to his community to join Congress in the fight for freedom and a year later propounded his theory of composite nationalism.[5]

Among the most vociferous mass contact campaigners in UP were several young and brilliant lawyers, journalists, teachers, poets, and writers. Most of them were educated either in Aligarh or in British universities. Having been tutored in Marxism-Leninism, they shared a common commitment to the revolutionary transformation of Indian society through an alliance with radical elements in Congress. They brought to bear a Marxist perspective on communalism that was markedly different from both the religious-oriented approach of the Khilafatists and that of the Congress. Muslims of Ansari's generation whose efforts to achieve Hindu-Muslim reconciliation found fruition merely in conferences, pacts, and short-term agreements. Nadera Begum, Munir Chowdhury, Ajit Guha, Ranesh Dasgupta and others rejected communal categories that they believed had been superimposed by the British to create fissures in the mass struggle and regarded any rapprochement with the self-styled leaders of the Muslim community as counter-productive. Congress, they argued, deserved support because it favoured abolition of the taluqdari system and liquidation of rural indebtedness and insisted on the relief for the landless and the unemployed. The Muslim League, in contrast, was allied with the British government and was engaged in promoting the interests of the privileged classes.[6] In 1940, Sher-e-Bangla A.K. Fazlul Haque tabled the historic Resolution incorporating the idea of more than one states in the Indian sub-continent. According to this resolution, there was to be a separate state comprising the different language speaking regions in the Indian sub-continent. But the plan was completely side-tracked when India was divided in 1947 on Jinnah's Two-nation Theory, and the artificial state of Pakistan came into being with two wings separated by a thousand miles.

Bengali Hindu cultural nationalism had begun to take shape, and this had an impact on the thoughts of at least a section of Bengali Muslims. Some of them struggled to identify themselves as Bengalis. Various questions pertaining to their language, literature, education, social problems and politics, which had already begun to agitate the Bengali Muslims, found expression in their writings.

In the late nineteenth century, there was no formal political organization for the Indian Muslims, though, Muslim politics was dominated by the Aligarh school. The partition of Bengal by Lord Curzon in 1905 formed the immediate background for the emergence of the Muslim League. Till then, the Muslims stayed away from politics, as per the advice of Syed Ahmed Khan. But, the partition of Bengal led to the creation of the new province of East Bengal and Assam, where the Muslims formed the majority, they got better chance of education and job opportunities. The nawab of Dhaka was catering much patronage and influence in the new province. The British authority, in fact, thrust informal leadership of the East Bengal Muslims upon the nawabs as a means to counter the swadeshi movement. Muslim political aspirations were aroused under such forces. Ratanlal Chakrobarty of Dhaka University in his book on the victims of the language movement points out that, like the Hindus, the Bengali Muslims could get their wards educated in English without detriment to their religious faith; the *moulvis* and *mollahs* were also taken to task for their failure to strike a balance between the traditional learning and English education. In reality, the system of education and opportunities in East Bengal, the sympathetic attitude of the colonial rulers towards the Muslim leaders and many other issues formed the background to the establishment of the Dhaka University.

As to the benefits they could derive from English education, it was generally held that it would help them in meeting their economic needs, particularly in getting employment in public services. Apprehension was expressed in the *Islam Pracharak* (1903) of the growing reluctance on the part of the English-educated Muslims to receive religious instruction from competent authorities or to study Islamic scriptures.

It is noteworthy in this context that the Nawab family of Dhaka played a crucial part in the formation of the All India Muslim League (1906) and a large number of upper class Muslims rallied round the Nawab family of Dhaka. Particular reference may be made about Nawab Salimullah of Dhaka Nawab family, and the book, *Amar Dekha Rajnitir Panchash Bachar*, written by Abul Mansur Ahmed or *Kaler Bhaley*, autobiography of Basanti Guha Thakurta, and similar other books, point out the intrigues of Bengali Muslims at that time.

Here in Calcutta, on December 2, 1906, a section of the anti-Partitionists founded an organization of their own in Calcutta, the Bengal Mohammedan Association. Abdul Rasul was made its president, Maulavi Ebrahim Mahomed and Maulavi Abdul Majeed its vice-presidents; Maulavi Abdul Kasem of Burdwan, Maulavi Mujibur Rahman and Abul Halim Ghuznavi respectively became its first secretary, joint secretary and treasurer. Maulana Akram Khan (1868-1968) was the publisher and editor of the Bengali weekly *Saptahik Muhammadi*; Maulavi Muniruzzaman Islamabadi, Khan Bahadur Maulami Mohammad Yusuf, Nawab Nasir Hussain, Maulavi Emad Ali Khan, Chaudhury Siddiqui Ahmed, Maulavi Dedar Bux, Noor Ismail took active interest in that association. Unlike the Bengal Provincial Muslim League, which was Urdu-oriented and communal in political tone, the Bengal Mohammedan Association stood for Bengali as the language of the Muslims and was strongly in favour of communal harmony in the struggle against the foreign ruler. It, in fact, projected a new political thought within the Bengali Muslim community. Its activities, however, were very limited. One may refer to the Shimla conference (1945) as the background to the organization of the upper class Muslim gentry.

At about this time Abdur Rasul and some of his close associates like Maulavi Abul Kasem of Burdwan, Maulavi Mujibur Rahman,

A.H. Ghuznavi urgently felt that a national and discerning English-language newspaper was needed for educating the English-knowing Muslim youths of the province. It would help them to think dispassionately on different trends within the community and to resolve the political conflicts within themselves, which had been sparked off by the partition. One may note in this context that the Muslim middle educated class was not a homogenous community, and tne British persuaded the policy of 'Divide and Rule', in organizing them. At the turn of the century, politics and society of Bengal was met with a convulsion in the clash between the emergence of national sentiment, and the attack of the British government on the nationalists through their weapon of partitioning the province. The policy of partition of Bengal (1905) was able to make a breakthrough to the long tradition of Hindu-Muslim political unity. In addition, an English-language Muslim weekly, they thought, would serve as a link between the articulate sections of the community scattered all over the country and thus bring about certain degree of political cohesion.

The anti-partitionists were critical about the policy of 'Divide and Rule' pursued by the government. *The Mussalman* condemned Lyon's Circular (May 25, 1906) making special provisions in favour of the Muslims in public services with the ulterior motive of alienating them from the popular cause and creating tension between the Hindus and Muslims. At the same time, however, the anti-partitionists did not hesitate to raise their voice of protests against instances of Hindu assumption of superiority. The most important result of the communal and separatist tendencies among the frustrated educated Muslims was the foundation of the All-India Muslim League in 1906 under the leadership of Aga Khan, the Nawab of Dhaka and Nawab Mohsin-ul-Mulk.

The Mussalman, in fact, came out with a long list of such grievances even while pleading for unity. In Bihar and the Central Provinces, the Wardha and Vidya Mandir schemes of education, the singing of the Bande Mataram song and the hoisting of the Congress flag were serious issues of communal mobilization. Added to these were local grievances: inadequate Muslim representation in certain branches of administration, discrimination in disbursing loans and educational grants, and minor but incredibly trivial issues such as withdrawal of the Jabalpur riot cases of 1938.[7]

The appeal of one group of politicians against partition however met with poor response from the Bengali Muslims and in a series of articles in the *Islam Pracharak* the anti-partitionists did not hesitate to raise their voice of protests against instances of Hindu assumption of superiority. Muslims were condemned as cowards or idiots. Even in the *Nava Nur* (1906) an article was published questioning the utility of Hindu-Muslim co-operation in politics. In the Simla Deputation to Lord Minto on October 1, 1906, the Aligarh-based Muslim elite group had already pleaded for separate electorates and representation in excess numerical strength for their contribution to the defence of the empire. So, the Government was requested to open agricultural banks for the cultivators and help Muslim traders to stock cheap consumer goods.

However, the forced resignation of Sir Bamfylde Fuller, the new Lieutenant Governor of Eastern Bengal and Assam (October 1905 to August 1906) who had been following frankly anti-Hindu policies, took the pro-partitionist Muslims by surprise and also alarmed them. On August 6, 1906 at the Dacca Muslim rally, which was one of the many protest rallies held throughout that province, Salimullah publicly regretted the action of the Viceroy.

Minto's reply to the Simla deputation of 1906 committed the British government to the principle of Separate Electorates for the benefit of the Muslims. The Regulations made under the Act of 1909 implemented this principle, i.e., seats were allotted to the Muslims on the communal basis. The first world war stimulated political aspirations in different quarters.

The reform proposals of changes in the Executive Council sent to London in 1907 by Minto went through substantial changes, in course of negotiations between the Secretary of State and the government of India, and in their changed form they provided the basis of the Indian Councils Act passed by the Parliament in 1909.

By 1912, the total number of Muslim teachers in the government and schools of all kinds had risen. Therefore, according to historians, the Muslim League now supported the partition of Bengal, demanded special safeguards for the Muslims in Government services and secured the acceptance of separate electorate for the Muslims from the Viceroy. In the hands of the British, the Muslim League became a major instrument in curbing the rising nationalist movement.

The overall percentage of Muslims in government services in East Bengal increased from 14.7 per cent in 1907 to 17.8 per cent in 1910. Again, in 1907 a sum of ₹ 3,50,000 was assigned by the Imperial government for the construction of the 'reverent', on the right bank of the river Karnafuli. In 1911 another sum of Rupees three lakhs was sanctioned for the improvement of the communication system. So, the government sanctioned ₹ 2,50, 000 as loans to the peasants of Mymensingh during 1908 and distributed them through those banks.

At a public meeting held at Calcutta Town Hall, upgrading of the status of the Calcutta *Madrassah* as a first grade degree college was demanded by Muslim citizens. However, there was an opposite trend also. In the meantime, as Dhaka became the headquarters of the provincial Muslim League, West Bengal Muslims founded a separate provincial office at Calcutta in January, 1909.

Moulvi Abdul Karim, the noted educationist, in his note submitted to the government-sponsored educational conference (February-March, 1908) at Dhaka, strongly opposed the introduction of Urdu as the mother-language of the Bengali Muslims. There was one section that was at least anti-Urdu. In the opinion of Bengali nationalist Muslims, there was a sense of oneness for being a part of Bengal. The President of the Eastern Bengal Provincial Mohamedan Conference at Bogra in March 1910, urged upon the Bengali Muslims the necessity to develop their literature with the help of Bengali. Meanwhile, constitutional reforms for India as proposed by Lord Morley and Minto was embodied in the Indian Councils Act of 1909. It gave a formal, constitutional recognition to the Muslims as a separate political community. It was the Aligarh school which readily provided leadership of the League.

The new phase in Jinnah's political career began in 1927 when, as President of the Muslim League, he endorsed a four-point-programme: 1. constitution of Sind, a Muslim-majority region in the Bombay Presidency, as a separate province; 2. introduction of Montague-Chelmsford reforms in three Muslim-majority provinces: Sindh, North-West Frontier Province and Baluchistan; 3. guarantee of Muslim majority in the Punjab and Bengal legislatures; 4. reservation of at least 1/3 of the seats in the central legislature or the Muslims who constituted about ¼ of India's total population. His purpose was to ensure Muslim dominance in five provinces and a strong position for Muslims at the center. This was a prelude to Jinnah's 'Fourteen Points' (1929), which covered much wider ground, and in the post-1937 period, Jinnah emerged as an inscrutable diplomat whose attitude had become harder towards the Congress.

In 1930, poet Iqbal had spoken of a Muslim state as a measure of cultural centralization of Islam in India in a specific territory. But Iqbal expected it to develop this within the 'body-politik of India' and his ideas inspired the Cambridge student Chowdhury Rahmat Ali to coin the word Pakistan. As for the Muslim masses, Ayesha Jalal has shown that, victorious Pakistan was not built on the unbroken crescendo of a mass movement. The Muslim popularity for a separate state took time to develop.

A splendid opportunity of building a united India was lost in 1927-8 and Jinnah engaged himself in legal practice in London, leaving behind the League organization in disarray. The central political figure at that time, Mohammed Ali Jinnah, a Bombay barrister, was educated in England. He began his political career as a liberal nationalist in association with Dadabhai Naoraji and Gopal Krishna Gokhale. He gave up his liberal ideology at the initial stage of the Gandhian era. His aristocratic mind was repelled by the non-co-operation movement because it made a direct appeal to the masses and brought politics to the open field. Jinnah's deep-rooted hostility to Gandhi was due to two factors: the 'Mahatma's' views on religion and morality, which implied close link between religion and politics, and his technique of 'satyagraha', which involved mass struggle against the British government. In later days however Jinnah himself used religion for political purposes.

The Communal Award of 1932 was the result of London's decision to divide power in the provinces among the rival communities and social groups which, in its view, constituted Indian society. A number of safeguards were designed to limit the scope of the greater 'autonomy'. According to Joya Chatterjee, the most striking feature of the Communal Award was its distribution of Hindu and Muslim seats.[8] For over a century, the British had ruled India by coming to terms with the interests of those whom they had identified as 'natural leaders' of the Indian society, balancing against one another and subordinating them all to their paramount purpose of maintaining

British rule in India.[9] At the same time, the British distrusted their motives. Through this contradictory contradiction, British rule sought to justify itself in theory and to sustain itself in practice: the colonial civilians claimed to act both as arbiters between the conflicting interests in Indian society and, at the same time, as the guardians of the people against the rapacity and corruption of their leaders.

The Communal Award reflected both the morality and the self-interest of this tradition. The legislatures both at the centre and in the provinces were to be carved up between various interests: Muslims, depressed classes, Sikhs, Europeans, and the 'General' population of Hindus, as well as the 'special' constituencies of landholders, workers, women and dons.[10] The seats allotted to each of these groups were intended to reflect the 'importance' more than mere numbers.[11] So in Bengal, of the 250 seats in the proposed Legislative Assembly, the European group, less than 1 per cent of Bengal population, were allotted 25 seats in all, or 10 per cent of the total. Elections to the Assembly, in addition, would be 'separate representation': Muslims alone would elect Muslims, Hindus would elect Hindus, and Europeans would elect Europeans.[12]

The whole situation turned upside down with the outbreak of the Second World war in 1939. In Bengal and Punjab, gradually the League received support from the influential heads of religious groups. The Muslim League had always been an urban-based political organization and its autocratic leaders had little contact with the masses. The name of religion and the services of the 'mullah's were freely utilized by the League. 'Volunteer corp's and 'national guard's were organized. The services of the 'khaksara's, a militant political party in the Punjab, was secured.

The League and its leader Jinnah were aware of the fact that, the provinces with majority and minority Muslims should both be safeguarded. In 1939, there was the first hint that the British might concede the demand for a separate Muslim state, if the Muslim League could grasp political power in the provinces at the time of election.

The Congress opposed the idea of dragging India into an imperial war, which would spell disaster on her resources. In October 10, 1939, the All India Congress Committee asked the British government to declare categorically that India would be made free after the war.

The propaganda of the Muslim League under the Suhrawardy

government raising the cry of the Pakistan movement, got hold specially the psychology of the educated Muslim community, with their large base at Dhaka. At the same time, after the thirties, the richer Muslim peasantry was obtaining a definite political objective. What happened therefore, was also a shift of the affluent and educated Mulims both in rural and urban areas, towards the Muslim League, living aside the '*Krishak Praja*' Party, which had formerly brought the Muslim community together in rural Bengal. Thus, the psychological tension of the Hindu '*bhadalok*' class was brought face-to-face with the rising affluent and educated Muslim community, leading ultimately to the struggle for power, in the '40s of the twentieth century.

The Lahore Resolution (1940) forwarded by A.K. Fazlul Haque of the Muslim League was quite vague on the issue of creation of a Muslim state. A.K. Fazlul Huq was one of the leading politicians of Bengal at this time. At that time, every famous person was comparable to an institution. There was the inception of parliamentary party politics, but it was not strong enough to keep the members within a chain. Fazlul Huq boycotted Muslim League in the year 1942 and a new ministry was formed, together with Hindu Mahasabha and Congress. Shyamaprasad Mukherjee was included inside the ministry and this was known as the 'Shyama-Huq Ministry'.

Lord Linlithgow gave the League friendly assurances and it was in that background that the League arrived at the Lahore Resolution of 1940. The All India Muslim League led by Jinnah adopted the historic Lahore Resolution of 23rd March, 1940, calling for the independence of Muslim-majority provinces, and within the short space of seven years, the ramshackle League created a movement and pushed it to a successful conclusion in 1947.

To secure the cooperation of Indians on a broad basis, it sent to India in March 1942 a mission headed by a Cabinet Minister, Sir Strafford Cripps who had earlier been a radical member of the Labour Party and a strong supporter of Indian national movement. The popular demands against the INA trials, the naval mutiny erupting peasant movements in all corners of India made the government uncertain whether the disaffected armed forces would be able to control the mass movements. Meanwhile politics was taking a different trend. Bipan Chandra points out that, the British government now desperately wanted the active cooperation of Indians in the war effort[13]. Cold-shouldering the League which seemed to hold out such a threat, the Cabinet Mission announced on 16th May 1946, that it had a revised three-tier plan and it had a stronger all-India center.

Having occupied Poland, Belgium, Holland, Norway and France in the west as well as most of Eastern Europe, Nazi Germany attacked the Soviet Union on 22 June 1941. On 7 December Japan launched a surprise attack on the American fleet at Pearl Harbour and joined the war on the side of Germany and Italy. It quickly overran the Phillipines, Indo-China, Indonesia, Malaya and Burma. It occupied Rangoon in March 1942. This brought the war to India's door-step.

By the end of the Second World war, the British came to realize that they could not keep the empire. All the Viceroys tried to decide how to do the transfer of power and to whom—both the Congress and the League had become powerful. The British government realized that the pressure of the war economy would be so great that Britain would be unable to maintain the Indian empire. Also in the 1940s Netaji Subhash Chandra Bose was trying to disrupt the empire with the help of Japan. Within India, the Indian nationalists were persistent in their demand for freedom. Taking everything into consideration, the Prime Minister Attlee on February 20, 1947, announced in the House of Commons that the British government shall leave India very soon, not later than June 1948. Formerly, in March 1946, a Cabinet Mission had been sent to India to settle all kinds of political deadlock. There was great expectation that the British government would be able to arrange for the transfer of power to the Indian leaders and there would be a federal government in India, including the native states. Further, a Constituent Assembly would be formed to frame a constitution for India and each province would have elections through an electorate divided into different communities, such as, general Muslims and Sikhs.

At the initial stage, the Cabinet Mission was accepted by the Muslim League. the Congress and the Sikhs, but when it was found that in the Constituent Assembly a large majority was enjoyed by the Congress, Jinnah backed out and dissociated himself from his commitment to the Cabinet Mission plan. After all this tiresome negotiations over the issue of transfer of power, the British government took the drastic decision of recalling Lord Wavell and sending Lord

Mountbatten to arrange for the transfer of power in India. He started negotiations with Indian leaders with a view to bring about a solution of the Indian problem agreeable to all political parties. He came to the conclusion that, a compromise between the Muslim League and the Congress could not be possible on the basis of a united India.

Throwing away all kinds of propriety, Jinnah called for Direct Action. The Labour government went on attempting to induce Congress to accept the grouping formula from June to December 1946. When Jawaharlal Nehru disavowed grouping, however, Jinnah angrily decreed a "day of action" on 16 August 1946, and on this day violence erupted in Calcutta that was not suppressed until after four thousand people had been killed.

The next question is about the Congress-Raj rapprochement and the popular Muslim upheaval—the great Kolkata killings of 1946 was a monstrous mass upheaval which had very little to do with the high politics of All India Muslim League, its roots being embedded in the simmering social turbulence of Calcutta underworld.

Seeing the danger of leaving the Centre to the Congress, Jinnah entered the interim government despite the fact that his demand for sole Muslim representation was set aside. He restored to the tactic of paralyzing the government and blocking any constitutional initiative. The League took the stand that the Congress acceptance of the Three-tier arrangement had been no more than a dishonest trick, and announced on 31st January 1947 that the Cabinet Mission Plan was dead.

Lord Mountbatten leaned openly towards the Congress and in the imperial negotiation that followed, popular currents in the Indo-Muslim political world, over which Jinnah had no control, swept the country towards Pakistan. The Muslim League's call for unionist ministry in Pakistan aroused deep-seated Hindu and Sikh fears, while the widely popular Islamic 'jehad' ensured the cornered League's survival.

In 1947, Bengal was partitioned again, following horrific clashes between Hindus and Muslims, and the partition was cut up to serve the requirements of independence of India from its colonial statehood. This time, vis-à-vis the partition of 1905, the partition of Bengal was preceded by an organized agitation, which demanded the vivisection of the province on the basis of religion. This movement was led by the very same section of Bengali society that had dominated its nationalist politics since early twentieth century: the so-called '*bhadralok*' or respectable people of Bengal. In less than forty years, '*bhadralok*' politics had come full circle, moving away from nationalist agenda to more parochial concerns. The central purpose of this work will be to explain these changes in '*bhadralok*' politics and to interpret their apparent shift towards 'communalism'.

The main thrust of the national movement was directed against British colonialism, but when in course of time it appealed to religion, it did so to mobilize religious sentiment against British rule. Communal parties and ideologies, always defined the community based on religion as a political unit which stood as adversaries in relation to other communities. In theory, therefore, communal ideologists owed more to the colonial tradition and ideas about India, than the nationalist. Not only did they see India as a society dominated by communities, just as colonial civil servants did, they also regarded the two main communities as being irreconcilably opposed to each other. It followed that communal parties were by no means necessarily hostile to the Raj and enjoyed its patronage.

By 1947, Britain's Home government felt so sick and tired of Hindu-Muslim conflicts, petty bickering and wrangling and was so preoccupied with its own post-War economic problems that Clement Attllee's cabinet decided to cut and run from its imperial albatross as swiftly as possible. In his first great speech to Pakistan's Constituent Assembly in Karachi on August 11, 1947, Jinnah said, "You are free; you are free to go to your temples, you are free to go to your mosques or to any other place of worship in this state of Pakistan ... You may belong to any religion or caste or creed...".[14]

Islam and Nationalism

Muslims constitute an *ummah* and *ummah* cannot be confined to any territorial limit.[15] However, Maulana Husain Ahmed Madani, the eminent Islamic theologian from India, maintained that nation is a geographic concept whereas *ummah* is a religious or spiritual concept. Muslims are *ummah* and in that sense, an international community. (The Islamic community, or *Umma*, to use the Quranic term, dates its foundation to a specific event in the life of Mohammed). But, the

Maulana says, one should not confuse between the concept of nation and that of *ummah*. The former is a political concept whereas the latter is a religious category.

Thus it is interesting to note that Maulana Husain Ahmed Madani who was also the president of the Jaim'at al-'Ulama-I-Hind', refused to support two nation theory propounded by Jinnah and his Muslim League.[16] Ayesha Jalal explains that Mohammed Ali Jinnah's self-attribution of sole spokesman ship of a constructed, "Muslim community" placed the Congress leadership in disarray.[17] Former deputy prime minister Lal Krishna Advani was perfectly right in his resent assessment of Pakistan's founding father and great leader Mohammed Ali Jinnah as a secular, tolerant leader, rather than a narrowly religious one.[18]

Jinnah was hailed by Mahatma Gandhi's political '*guru*', Congress president, Gopal Krishna Gokhale, as India's "best ambassador of Hindu-Muslim unity".[19] Stanley Wolpert points out that, Jinnah was born a Muslim and remained so throughout his life, he feared that British India's Muslim minority would have to face greater hardships and more discrimination under a potential "Hindu Raj" than they had hitherto faced under the British.[20] In the aftermath of the 1937 elections he hoped that Jawaharlal Nehru's victorious Congress might generously respond to overtures from his Muslim League to form coalition governments in several of the large provinces, particularly UP.[21]

Notes

1. Sibnarayan Ray *Bengal Renaissance The First Phase*, p. 19.
2. Chandi Prasad Sarkar, *The Bengali Muslims A Study in their Politicization (1912-1919)*, p. 4.
3. *Ibid.*, p. 4.
4. Mushirul Hasan, 'The Muslim Mass Contacts Campaign', p. 132.
5. *Ibid.*, p. 146.
6. *Ibid.*, p. 144.
7. Mushirul Hasan, *Themes in Indian History India's Partition Process, Strategy and Mobilization*, p. 18.
8. Joya Chatterji, *Bengal Divided Hindu Communalism and Partition 1932-47*, p. 19.

9. *Ibid.*, p. 19.
10. Joya Chatterjee, *Bengal Divided: Hindu Communalism and Partition*, p. 19.
11. *Ibid.*, p. 19.
12. *Ibid.*, p. 19.
13. *Modern India* (National Council of Educational Research and Training) p. 298.
14. *Ibid.*, p. 23.
15. Asghar Ali Engineer 'Islam and Nationalism', paper presented at 'National Seminar on Indian Nationalism'
16. *Ibid.*, p. 1.
17. Ayesha Jalal, *The Sole Spokesman Jinnah, the Muslim League and the demand for Pakistan* (1985).
18. Stanley Wolpert, 'Faithfully Secular', *India Today*, (June 27, 2005), p. 22.
19. *Ibid.*, p. 22.
20. *Ibid.*, p. 22.
21. *Ibid.*, p. 23.

3

Historiography on the Partition of Bengal

Why a historiography is necessary: For a total understanding of a time of turmoil in a colonial state, where partition is taking place twice within a time span of less than thirty years, opinion of scholars should be ascertained. This chapter covers only a brief survey of the relevant opinion of historians on the second partition of East Bengal, because as such it is an oceanic task to survey all the writings on the subject.

First and foremost is Joya Chatterjee's book, *Bengal Divided Hindu Communalism and Partition, 1932-1947* concentrates upon the Hindu *bhadralok* class of Bengal, who dominated nationalist politics in the province of East Bengal. According to Chatterji, these politics that always had a narrow social base in Bengal, and support from the masses, even in the heyday of Gandhi's influence, was limited and sporadic. Except for a brief interlude during the Khilafat agitation, the Muslims of Bengal, who were more than half the population of the province, kept away from the movements led by the bhadralok. However, despite being overwhelmingly bhadralok in character, the Bengal Congress remained a political force to be reckoned with until well into the 1920s, and during the first three decades of the twentieth century exerted a powerful influence over the mainstream of Indian nationalism.

In the twentieth century, *bhadralok* identity came to rest increasingly upon a perception of itself as a cultured and enlightened class, heir to the traditions of the 'Bengal Renaissance', and bearer of progress and modernity. This self-image informed *bhadralok* politics, justifying the claim for representation by early nationalists. In later years, it also served to justify the demand that Hindus should continue to dominate Bengal, and ultimately that Bengal be partitioned.

The timidity that characterized nationalist mobilization in rural Bengal was an expression of the same predicament. Notwithstanding the fact that it was led by the avowedly 'modern' progressive and anglicized, *bhadralok* nationalism drew inspiration, to quite a remarkable extent, from Hindu 'revivalist' ideologies, emphasizing religious precepts. Thus Aurobindo Ghosh, packed off to England at the age of seven and educated in London and Cambridge, developed the philosophy of 'political Vedanta', which preached the identification of the nation with the mother Goddess Kali. When he returned home, while Bepin Chandra Pal and Sarala Debi, both from old Brahmo families, introduced Kali Puja and Shivaji festivals onto the nationalist agenda. Bengal's terrorist organizations, though they found their recruits mainly among the western educated, bound their young followers with religious vows inspired by Sakta philosophy. Even Chittaranjan Das, who gave the appearance of being thoroughly 'anglicized', was deeply influenced by Vaisnavism and has made significant contributions to Vaisnava mystic poetry, while his young lieutenant Subhas Bose was a disciple of Ramkrishna and Swami Vivekananda. This suggests that an uncritical use of the notion of 'westernisation' to explain Bengal's social history has many pitfalls, and that accepting *bhadralok* descriptions of themselves as the fuglemen of modernity and progress is unwise. *Bhadralok* lifestyles more usually reflected a mix of 'modernity' and 'tradition', in which outward mannerisms of speech and dress often co-existed uneasily with a deeper 'orthodoxy' in the more private and fundamental concerns of family life and morality. The same ambivalence characterized their political philosophy, which typically asserted the greatness of the Hindu spiritual tradition even as it acknowledged the technological and political prowess of Europe.

Bhadralok leaders saw themselves as the standard-bearers of Hindu Bengal's destiny. This was a theme that was to re-emerge powerfully in the Hindu propaganda that accompanied the agitation for the partition of Bengal in 1946-7. The description of the *bhadralok* as a 'westernized elite' is perhaps an uncertain guide to understanding the political preoccupations, or to unraveling the complexities and contradictions of the political philosophies to which they subscribed.

Many of the idioms of Hindu communal discourse were thus recognized in nationalist and indeed the thought of the Bengal Renaissance, and had been common currency since the beginning of the twentieth century. But they were subtly reworked in the following decades, their emphasis shifting from anti-British themes to an anti-Muslim posture. Jaya Chatterjee's work seeks to understand this reorientation of the *bhadralok* political perceptions within a context profoundly influenced by changes that transformed Bengali society and politics during the last fifteen years of the Raj.

The reorientation of the Bengal Congress, 1937-45, examines the declining role of the Bengal Congress in all-India politics, its changing relationship with the central Congress leadership, the emergence within the party of 'right' -and -'left' wing groupings, and the increasing preoccupation of the Bengal Congress with parochial issues. The eventual capture of the organization by those on the right who stood for the defenses of 'Hindu' interests, and the emasculation of the left within the party, suggested a profound change in political priorities and perceptions of the *bhadralok.*

As 'Muslim rule' came to be regarded as the great and immediate threat to Hindu society, the *bhadralok* reappraised their past and gave the British the role of liberators who freed Hindu Bengal from Muslim tyranny. Loyalty again became a respectable badge for the Bengali babu: indeed the inglorious history of *bhadralok* collaboration with British rule was now proudly recalled in order to strengthen the case for special consideration from a *Raj*, which threatened to abandon them to the very tyrants from whom they had been rescued. At the same time, the *bhadralok* perception of themselves as a cultured elite acquired a new significance: it now promoted a powerful sense of cultural superiority over the Muslims of Bengal.

By 1929, the British policy-makers in London and New Delhi could see that the constitutional arrangements devised by Montagu and Chelmsford ten years before would have to be reviewed. The pressures of the past decade had brought constitutional change back upon the political agenda. 'Provincial autonomy', was devised as a measure to resist pressure at the center by nationalist politicians, while at the same time broadening the base of Indian collaboration with the *Raj.*

"In the late 1930s and 1940s, *bhadralok* politics underwent changes that corresponded, in interesting ways, with the ideological shifts that have been discussed"[1], in the issue of the construction of *bhadralok* communal identity. Most marked was the tendency to shun high nationalist endeavour and to focus instead on narrower, more immediate concerns. Perhaps the most ambitious scheme to attract the energies of the *bhadralok* in these years was the attempt to forge a greater Hindu political community, uniting the disparate states and tribes of the putative 'Hindu family' into a single harmonious whole. But, generally, *bhadralok* politics grew more parochial, increasingly confined to the petty manouverings of the localities and District Boards. This trend was particularly marked in traditional *bhadralok* strongholds in the west Bengal heartland where a growing Muslim influence had begun to erode established patterns of dominance.

The book, *Bengal Divided Hindu Communalism and Partition 1932-1947*, published in 1995, has viewed the background to the partition of Bengal, 1947, in a rather unique way, and has put forward the thesis that the Hindu '*bhadralok*' class was no less responsible for the partition, than the Muslims of Bengal. Joya Chatterji says, "Partition is generally believed to have been a consequence of the separatist politics of Muslim minorities, but in the case of Bengal, Hindus evolved a parallel separatism of their own".[2] In *Bengal Divided*, Chatterji argues that, Bengal was not really "a hapless pawn in the end-games of empire, but rather, the *bhadralok* Bengalis had really wanted a separate homeland of their own, to the exclusion of the Muslims". On the contrary, "partition was not imposed by the center on an unwilling province."

In the book, *Bengal Divided*, it has been pointed out that, large section of Bengali literature, from Bankimchandra Chattopadhyay, Rabindranath Tagore and others, have fully been used to depict the identity of the Bengali '*bhadralok*', who were the torch-bearers of movement for liberation of the country from foreign yoke. But the author has specially pinned her thoughts on Saratchandra Chattopadhyay, whose novels like *Pather Dabi* and *Biprodas*, has been extensively used to depict the identity of the Bengali *bhadralok*, who were torch-bearers of movement for liberation of the country from foreign yoke. But the author has specially pinned her thoughts on Saratchandra Chattopadhyay, whose novels like *Pather Dabi* and *Biprodas*, has been extensively used to show the formation of the *bhadralok* identity in the Hindu society.

Rabindranath Tagore's '*Gora*', Bankimchandra Chattopadhyay's *Amarnath* (*Rajani*) and Saratchandra Chattopadhyay's *Sabyaschi*, *Biprodas* and other personalities are analysed and presented in a manner, which indicate the formation of Hindu '*bhadralok*' identity in the early twentieth century. Various aspects of the '*bhadralok*'hero are brought out in an exemplary manner. The author suggests that, the position and consolidation of the '*bhadralok*' in the Hindu society is reflected through the literature of the time. It is this '*bhadralok*' class which took the lead in the socio-political condition of the Bengali society and prepared the ground for Hindu-Muslim separatism.

In the 20s of the twentieth century, after the failure of the non-co-operation, *Khilafat* and other political movements, Saratchandra Chattopadhyay declared in his '*Bartamaan Hindu Musalman Shamasya* ', that Hindus and Muslims are not equals and unity cannot exist between them. Saratchandra Chattopadhyay mainly emphasizes that the culture of the Hindu *bhadralok* cannot embrace the *Mussalman*s, who thereby are inferior to them, specially because the Bengali Muslims are largely converted. Joya Chatterji argues that the symbol of '*bhadralok*' culture gradually developed a particular political identity and also a symbol of communal identity of all Hindus. It overlooked the fact that millions of poor, low-caste and uneducated Hindus remained outside the periphery of the '*bhadralok* society. Chatterji brings down her dissertation upon the writings of Sir Jadunath Sarkar, who spoke highly of the Renaissance of the elitist culture, that was the result of the British rule in Bengal, and denied the Muslims a place in the history of Bengal. According to him, the Muslim period was a dark age of unbelievable tyranny. The exceptions to this line of thinking, she says, was Akshyay Kumar Maitro, writer of *Sirajuddaulah*, and Subhash Chandra Bose, who, in *An Indian Pilgrim* (1937), presented the battle of Plassey, as an instance of Hindu-Muslim co-operation against a common enemy. However, it is the *bhadralok* culture which ultimately gained acceptance.

It is true, as Joya Chatterji points out, Bengal society mainly reflected the '*bhadralok*' culture of Hindu community and they were eager to have a state of their own. But it is also true that, in the colonial period, after the failure of the *wahabi* movement, there was hardly any possibility of a movement for regeneration and reconstitution of the Muslim masses. The Muslim leadership in Bengal, from after

1906, was quite eager to court the British government. Whatever the contradictions of the Hindu *bhadralok* class, they had to build up a kind of nationalist identity, with its base in Bengal. Whether there was any such nationalist weakness on the part of the Muslims of Bengal, or they considered Bengal as their motherland, is not yet known. If, taking the chance of the vacuum created by the negative attitude of the Muslims, who failed to think of Bengal as their motherland, the Hindu '*bhadralok*' community, came heavily down upon Bengal politics. That was only natural. It may be mentioned that the Muslims of India were actually divided and sub-divided into small groups among themselves—Deoband, Ahmedia, Sufi, Sunni etc., so that, social unity was hardly possible among them and the British could become the only solid entity in their imagination.

Partha Chatterjee has shown, ('Bengal Politics and the Muslim masses' edited by Musirul Hassan), the process of uplift of the Muslim peasantry in the pre-dominantly Muslim districts of Bengal. Religion was always "sustaining an ideology of community solidarity", among the Muslim peasants in Bengal. And this had its effect in certain districts of northern and central Bengal, where a large part of Muslim cultivators were gradually getting rich and becoming owners of large holdings of rural lands. And, this had its effect on certain districts of northern and central Bengal, where a large part of Muslim cultivators were gradually getting rich and becoming owners of large holdings of rural lands. He says that, in Khulna, Noakhali and Tiperra, the well-to-do Mohammedan cultivators were forming a substantial community, few even acquiring the status of zamindars and rent-receivers, or acting as '*byapari*'s, i.e., agents in the jute and other kinds of trades. The situation was different in Dhaka and Faridpur, where there were few cases of cultivators rising into wealth and prosperity. In Dhaka division and east Bengal proper, there existed a rich Hindu landlord community belonging to a higher social category than the poor Muslim peasantry, the '*paschima*', i.e., Marwari moneylenders, who were active in jute-growing districts of Bengal. Taking everything together, there existed a situation of political confrontation, where Hindu landlords, traders and professionals in the towns, stood in sharp contrast with a well-off Muslim peasantry, active in the rural areas. This sometimes created a situation of riot, as in Pabna in 1926. Chatterjee thinks that, deep down in the nature of Muslim peasant consciousness, religion acted as a propelling factor, and after the death of the veteran Chittaranjan Das, who had provided a Hindu Pact, the rupture between the two communities became too evident. Almost in the same tune with Jaya Chatterji, but from a different angle, Partha Chatterjee points out that the Calcutta-based professional and business elite, representing the upper-caste Hindu '*bahdralok*', rentier classes, "now under considerable economic pressure, and, using the ... support of the revolutionary groups", ousted the Muslims from district leadership of various organizations in various districts of Bengal. Within the provincial Congress, the members largely spoke and voted in support of the rights of landlords, while the Muslim members lost their ground in speaking in favour of the tenants (1928). From now on, in the 1930s, the Muslim masses in Bengal decisively moved away from the Congress, and the Muslims participated in the civil disobedience movement in a small way.

Ratanlal Chakrobarty studies the problem of peasant indebtedness, particularly in the crucial decades, the 1930s and 1940s, time that witnessed the Great Depression, the emergence of war economy, the disastrous famine of 1943 and other developments.[3] The Bengal peasant was always in debt. To add to his misfortune, the great depression hit him hardest; he was then overburdened with debt. But as he was enfranchised and became politically important, his cause was taken up by politicians, the Government was prevailed upon to enact the Bengal Agricultural Debtors Act of 1935 providing for scaling down the debts through mutual agreement between the creditor and the debtor under the auspices of the Debt Settlement Board.

The operation of the Act led to a flight of capital from rural credit market to urban centers and consequently, to large-scale alienation of peasant holdings. These unwelcome and unexpected outcomes persuaded the authorities to terminate the ill-started experiment in 1945. Ratanlal Chakrobarty makes serious investigation into agricultural finance and rural credit of Bengal. (By Bengal, Ratanlal Chakrobarty meant what is now Bangladesh and West Bengal excluding the district of Sylhet). J.C. Jack in his book, *Economic Life of a Bengal District* (1916), undertook the arduous task of inquiring into household finance in the district of Faridpur along with his survey and settlement operations during the years 1906-1910.

S.C. Ray compiled *Agricultural Indebtedness in India and its*

Remedies in 1915 which dealt largely with official records on the problem and solution of rural indebtedness.[4] According to Ratanlal Chakrobarty, the Survey and Settlement Reports of the Bengal Districts from 1910 to 1930s throw great deal light on rural indebtedness. Among these reports F.D. Ascoli's *Dacca*, 1910-17; F.O. Bell's *Dinajpur*, 1934-40; S.N. Ray's *Hooghly*, 1930-37; F.W. Robertson's Bankura 1917-24; M.A. Momen's *Jessore*, 1920-24; F.A. Sachase's *Mymensingh* 1908-19 are of special importance. However, from 1925 onward, a number of economic enquiries were undertaken by the Central and Provincial Governments. The Royal Commission on Agriculture in 1928 largely dealt with the finance of agriculture. It collected oral and written statements from educationists, officials, economists and concerned people about rural finance.

The Economic Enquiry in the Rangpur District was conducted by the Settlement department. It looked at the economic condition in 11 villages of 508 families and found them in "a more serious condition of indebtedness than found in Faridpur by Jack".[5] The Bengal Provincial Banking Enquiry Committee was set up in 1929 with a view to investigating the condition of banking and to make recommendations for their improvement and expansion. The Committee conducted a comprehensive enquiry into rural finance with the following objects:

(i) to recommend ways and means for enabling the rural population to secure credit for improvement of land;
(ii) to suggest ways and means to "stimulate the habit of investment and attract banking deposits".[6]

The next important and comprehensive enquiry on all-Bengal-plan was conducted by the *Bengal Board of Economic Enquiry* in 1934. According to Ratanlal Chakrobarty, the Bengal Agricultural Debtors Act was enacted on the basis of some of the random enquiries conducted by the Board of Economic Enquiry. But the investigations of the Board of Economic Enquiry primarily dealt with the riot class and with special reference to their debts.

The selection of villages and families which were considered by the local officers as 'typical' minimized the statistical value of enquiry.[7] Besides, in selecting the riot class families, the distressed section of cultivators were practically excluded from the scope of enquiry. It is well-known that during the years of economic depression.

the riots, who had just enough to carry on, had been gradually selling out their lands. Consequently, during investigation of the Board of Economic Enquiry, many of these riots had become primarily under-riots or agricultural labourers with perhaps a small area of land still held as riots. These families were therefore excluded in selecting riot class of agriculturalists. The second enquiry, which was conducted more carefully, disclosed some surplus in several cases. The data could not, therefore, form the basis of any conclusion regarding the economic condition of the cultivators as such. But the Bengal Relief of Indebtedness Bill was based on this enquiry.

Another important work on rural finance was done by K.G. Shivaswamy.[8] His study entitled *Legislative Protection and Relief of Agricultural Debtors in India* was extended to the whole of India and a considerable portion was devoted to the legislative measures undertaken by the government of Bengal. He discussed the tenancy legislations restricting transfer of land in repayment of loan, and restricting the period of mortgages; the Bengal Money-lenders Act controlling the usurious system of money-lending and finally the Bengal Agricultural Debtors Act providing exclusive provision for scaling down of debts.

The Land Revenue Commission, known as Flood Commission, started its investigation at a time when the Bengal Agricultural Debtors Act was in operation. According to Ratanlal Chakrobarty, the Land Revenue Board examined the operation of the Bengal Agricultural Debtors Act and the introduction of the money-lenders Bill and its impact on the rural economy of Bengal.

The Constitutional reforms under the India Act of 1935 raised the status of the peasantry politically. According to Ratanlal Chakrobarty, to overcome the depression crisis and also to satisfy the pro-peasant lobbies the government enacted Bengal Debtors Act of 1935.[9] This Act embodied the recommendations of the Board of Economic Enquiry which was previously set up to investigate into the economic ailments and make remedial recommendations.

The Language Movement

A large number of very powerful authors leapt into prominence to describe the condition of Pakistan after the nation was born in 1947. Most of these writers wrote in Bengali, and dealt with different issues.

Abul Hashim in his book, *Amar jibon o bibhagpurbo bangladesher rajnity*, concentrates on the role of Fazlul Huq in the events immediately before and after the partition of Bengal.

A few weeks before the decline of the Muslim League government in Bengal, the election of members to Bardhaman provincial council came to an end. Abul Hashim in his book, *Amar Jibon o bibhagpurbo bangladesher rajnity*, points out that the Congress was a minority amongst the elected members and the district Muslim League occupied five seats.

The three volumes, *Bangladesher Itihash* (volume one: political history; volume two economic history; volume three: social and cultural history) edited by Sirajul Islam deals exhaustively on the different aspects of Bengal's history between 1707 and 1971. In his 'Introduction' he points out how the scholars have dealt with the problems of communalism and separatism, after 1947. Muslim nationalist leaders offering communal statistics reveal the discrimination between the Hindus and Muslims in the service sector, but remaining silent on the issue of communal education. He states that, there were few suitable candidates for a responsible post, compared to the Hindu candidates. The Muslim nationalist leaders also published long lists of statistics in different newspapers, showing the huge difference between Hindus and Muslims in the service sector and these pamphlets were distributed among the common people.

The volume on the political history of Bangladesh, 1707-1971, consists of twenty articles, the first fourteen of which deal with the different aspects of Bengal polity till the early twentieth century. The fifteenth essay by Harun Ar Rashid speaks of the enterprise to create an undivided, independent nation-state. He points out that in the changed circumstances of the post-Second World War, the end of British colonial rule became inevitable, since the colonized states eagerly wanted independence. British Prime Minister Attlee definitely announced that, Britain wanted to shake off its hands from India by 1948, and within that time-frame if the two parties, the Congress and the Muslim League, failed to come to any understanding, then India would be partitioned and Pakistan would be created. 'Transfer of Power Papers' and 'Mountbatten Papers' of the contemporary period, reveals the attitude of the British colonial rulers towards the establishment of an undivided, independent Bengal state.

He postulates that, the 'Suhrawardy-Hashim group' in the 1940s projected the scheme of 'Independent East Pakistan' or a 'Greater Bengal', which dealt with long-term questions, such as the idea of a united Bengal, or, Hindu-Muslim relationships within and outside Bengal. Rashid thinks that the project would have been successful, if the Bengali Hindus and the Muslims could unite in support of the central leaders. It was necessary to have a strong and transparent idea of Bengali nationalism, indiscriminate of Hindu-Muslim divide, but this was absent. In the contemporary socio-economic framework, it was a difficult task to construct a sense of Bengali nationalism, considering the socio-political ambition and social outlook of the two communities.

Badruddin Umar's books entitled, *Purba Banglar Bhasha Andolon o Tatkalin Rajnity* places emphasis on the language movement, which, he thinks, became the crucial issue of conflict between East and West Pakistan after the sovereign and independent states of India and Pakistan were established. In his article on language movement, he indicates that even before the state of Pakistan was established in August, 1947, a demand was made to make Bengali one of the state-languages in Pakistan while subsequently, as Badruddin Umar shows, the main person who propagated the idea was Hazlur Rehman, who was a central minister and a representative of Bengal as well, immediately after the partition of the province. He propagated through his speeches and messages in assemblies, the necessity of introducing Arabic script in the Bengali language; to create significant unity and strong bonds between the people of the two regions, and said that the script of all languages in Pakistan should be uniform. This conspiracy for changing the script started developing in the year 1949. Then from 18 April 1950, through the initiative of the central educational board, the preliminary part of imparting primary education to the adults started at twenty centers in different districts. A '*Dainik Azad*' report of 15 July, 1948 remarked that, 25 to 35 students started taking lessons in every educational institute in that way, and they would be engaged to receive education in those centers for three months.

Muhammad Shahidullah of, "*Purba Bangla Bhasha Shangshkar* Committee", was against the policy of imparting education through Arabic script. Earlier, in September, "*Purba Bangla Bhasha*

Committee", under the leadership of Maulana Akram Khan, in its report prescribed the postponement of writing the Bengali language in Arabic script by twenty years, and Muhammad Shahidullah now in his speech drew the attention of the government as also of the ordinary people towards this recommendation. Inspite of all these, the conspiracy of the Pakistan government to change the Bengali script remained unimpaired for some time. Some groups even wanted to make Arabic the state-language of Pakistan. However, as there was no particular pressure in contemporary educational circles regarding this proposal, it was not implemented further. Since this demand was related to the question of the development of Islamic culture, it indirectly made the introduction of Arabic script in Bengali language and making Urdu the state language, more forceful.

Apart from the language movement, Badruddin Umar focuses his attention on the growth of leftist politics in Bangladesh. There was an attempt to make some transformations in the language, in the name of reforming Bengali. A committee named 'East Bengal Language Committee', was created on 9 March, 1949, by the East Bengal government. Maulana Akram Khan was the Chairman of this committee and the members included Mohammed Shahidullah, Habibullah Bahar, Moazzem Hossain etc. This committee gave a final shape to their report on language policy and the Chairman of the Committee, Maulana Akram Khan, sent it to the educational Secretary, East Bengal government.

Musa Ansari deals with the role of the leftists in Bangladesh, and points out that, the 'Communist Krishak Sabha' had a special role to play in Bengal's nationalist movement. The Bombay party's central committee held a meeting in 1947 in midst of the worst riots of the twentieth century and it decided to unite the progressive forces within the country through the realization of democratic movements. The Communist Party celebrated the Independence Day together with the Congress and the Muslim League. According to 'Swadhinata', the representative of Indian Communist Party, the language movement was mainly directed by the Communist Party.

From the beginning of the language movement, Shahidullah Kaiser represented the Communist Party, but other than him, the other members—Nadera Begum, Munir Chowdhury, Ajit Guha, Ranesh Dasgupta, Sardar Fazlul Karim and many others were active in different phases of the language movement. As Umar thinks, one consequence of the language movement was the growth of democratic spirit among the students of East Bengal and the East Pakistan Students' Union was created by the non-communal, non-imperialist radical students. They were the predecessors of the Students Federation and the East Pakistan Communist Party decided to participate in different movements, under the banner of the Awami Muslim League.

Broadly, there are four schools of writers who deal with the history of Pakistan from 1947 to 1971. In the first place, there are the historians from the western world, such as the 'Oxford' or 'Cambridge' school, who look at the problem as a kind of political unrest in south Asia, and the breakup of the entire subcontinent. They also distinguish the part played by the foreign powers in the emancipation of a new nation, and the emergence of India as a stronghold in the subcontinent. Secondly, we may consider the viewpoint of West Pakistani military generals, who see the freedom struggle of the East Pakistanis as a betrayal to Muslim brotherhood and of the servitude of Muslim nationalism to Bengali nationalist feelings. The viewpoint of General G.W. Chowdhury in the book, *The Last Days of United Pakistan* (1974), may be an illustration of this school of thought. The third school of thought may be termed as the nationalist history of Bangladesh, where the writers of Bengali origin, either Muslims or Hindus from Bangladesh, deal with the process of struggle of East Pakistan against the colonial domination of the West Pakistanis. They mostly have a leftist orientation, and they deal mainly with the language movement, the rule of the military dictators and the struggle of the Bengali Muslims for gaining independence from western colonialism. In the final phase, there are the documents of different writers, who have tried to compile the reports from newspapers, electoral violence, and oral history of the independence and post-independence era. A huge amount of literature has been preserved mostly as secondary document in the books published by Sukumar Biswas, Ratanlal Chakrobarty and many others, in the Bangla Academy library of Dhaka etc.

As for the writers with a 'nationalist' viewpoint, in tracing out the political basis of nationalism, Azizur Rahman Mallick and Anwar Hussain maintain that, the rise of Bangladesh in 1971 symbolised the announcement of a distinct national identity, by terminating decades-old supremacy of West Pakistan. When a portion of a large population earns this kind of nationalism, it is termed as a "multi-dimensional phenomenon". These authors are of the opinion that, the nationalism that gave birth to Bangladesh, had its primary roots within the language and symbolized a distinct identity of the Bengalis. In a broad way, the sense of Bengali identity was the anti-thesis of Muslim nationalism created by Pakistan.

In the final chapter of the second volume of *Bangladesher Itihash*, (Economic History), Rehman Sobhan narrates his views on the expansion of Bengali nationalism between 1947 and 1971. Although the Bengalis of East Bengal were Pakistanis at that time, he admits that the history of Bengali national consciousness expanded over the past centuries, the first manifestation of which came out through the struggle of the Bengali Muslims for Pakistan.

Ratanlal Chakrobarty points out that, the Bengal Agricultural Debtors Act prescribed the liquidation of rural debts without any provision for maintaining the flow of credit. The existing institutional financing was too inadequate to meet the limited credit requirements. It seems that while formulating policies the government was guided more by political considerations than by economic principles. According to Chakrobarty,[10] Debtors Act were set up more for political gains than for economic recovery.

In 1944-5, the Government of Bengal sponsored a plot survey of the entire land of Bengal under the direction of H.S.M. Ishaque. Along with this agricultural census, H.S.M. Ishaque conducted an economic survey of 77 randomly selected villages of Bengal. Ratanlal Chakrobarty points out that, Sirajul Islam's article on, the Bengal Peasantry in Debt, though a sketchy one, covers nearly the entire period of the present study. It began with the Co-operative Societies Act and concluded in 1950s when the Debt Settlement Boards were officially wound up.

Professor Binay Bhushan Chaudhuri's article on, "The process of Depeasantisation in Bengal and Bihar, 1885-1947", dealt with debt question quite in details. He emphasized land transfers, price movements and large scale emergence of bargadari system.[11] Similarly, his another article on "The Land Market in Eastern India, 1793-1940", Part-I has dealt to some extent with the debt settlement operation and held it responsible for large scale land sale in Bengal.[12] Professor Sugata Bose in his Ph.D. thesis on "Agrarian Bengal" has devoted one chapter to the discussion of rural credit. He has also examined the impact of the credit crisis on the highly monetised economy of Bengal.

The economy of Bengal suffered a tumultuous jolt due to the collapse of the jute market during depression. It also affected the political situation to a large extent. It added a new dimension to peasant politics which was crystallized into an anti-landlord and anti-moneylender movement. In the face of mounting demands for restoration of peasant rights, the Bengal Tenancy Act, 1885 was amended giving peasants the right to transfer their holdings. It created a new problem.

The voluntary method existed in Bengal, Assam, the Punjab, Central Provinces and Madras. Earlier the system of amicable settlement had been tried at Chandpur where voluntary Debt Conciliation Boards were set up before the Bengal Agricultural Debtors Act was enacted and settled within one and half years time, the claims amounting to over 11 lakhs of which the creditors received a settlement about 3 lakhs in cash or kind.[13]

To deal with the problem of rural indebtedness, the Government of Bengal, however, created a special department. The Credit Branch of the Co-operative Credit Department was originally the office of the R.D.C. (Rural Development Commissioner) of the Bengal Secretariat. The Rural Indebtedness Branch took over the administration of the Bengal Agricultural Debtors Act from the R.D.C.'s office and became a full-fledged branch of Secretariat Department but without any Head of the Department subordinate to it. There were four Deputy Directors under the Branch who were assisted by 177 Special Debt Conciliation Officers for inspecting Debt Settlement Boards of which maximum number was about 5,000 stationed all over the province. This Rural Indebtedness Branch would control its own budget, and run its administration. However, with the reorganization of the Secretariat Offices in 1945, as a result of the recommendation of the Rowland's Committee, this Rural Indebtedness Branch was renamed as the Credit Branch of the new Department of Co-operation, Credit and Relief.

At this stage, a feeling of economic discrimination filled up the

Bengali psychology, the first manifestation of which came through the struggle of the Bengali Muslims for autonomy in East Pakistan. The Pakistan government failed to discard feeling of relative discrimination from the psychology of the people of East Bengal and this failure strengthened the Bengali nationalist forces between 1947 and 1971. It helped the rise of independent Bangladesh in 1971. Rehman Sobhan argues that, till the year 1947, the ordinary people of East Bengal specially the Bengali Muslims, considered themselves to be in a worse position than their counterparts, the Hindus of West Bengal. The Hindus were much better off, since West Bengal was more progressive. Working with such precepts in mind, the Bengali Muslims proceeded to get hold of an administrative system, where they could establish political preponderance. They wanted proprietary right over the land, to improve the education with the help of the state, to develop infrastructural industry in East Bengal and to industrialise the region.

The Sikhs from west Pakistan region had created a vacuum in the business world, and the ambitious Muslim businessmen from Pakistan wanted to fill in the vacuum themselves. Although communal riots took place in East Bengal, the Hindus and the Marwaris, who had control over the local economy, did not feel inclined to leave the area.

It was repeatedly said by the west Pakistani people—non-Bengali and Urdu—speaking, since the size of the market was great in West Pakistan than in the east, economic progress would take place there more naturally. In West Pakistan, the revenue expenditure included that for the central administration and for those working in defence, and for the production of power plants, telelinks and road-construction. It actually benefited urban life and helped crating the cities of Karachi, Rawalpindi and the new national capital, Islamabad. These expenditures incurred by the central government made private investment more active, since it created demand for commodities in West Pakistan, and it were the west Pakistan business community that were benefited from such investment. According to Rehman Sobhan, the main reason for political conflict between East and West Pakistan was the discriminatory policy of the government in development expenditure.

The third volume of *Bangladesher Itihash*, deals with the history of society and culture. In the introduction, Sirajul Islam argues that although the Hindu 'Bhadralok' class prepared for the 'Rakhi' ceremony in 1905 to maintain national unity, the same community agreed to the breakup of Bengal on communal lines. He further comments that, although decisions were taken by the Hindu 'Bhadralok' class in 1905 to maintain national unity, the same community agreed to the breakup of Bengal on communal lines. These had to be rectified in 1947 and similarly the 'Pakistan' decision of 1947 was corrected by the Bengali Muslim higher classes in the 1960s.

He alleges that the Muslim middle class accepted the proposal for partition and the imperialist British rulers were the manipulators of this process. When the British came to power, they had gained a large, unified province of Bengal and during the transfer of power, they divided it into two parts on the basis of communalism. The Hindu 'Bhadralok's got exemption from Muslim political domination and in other regions, the Muslims got exemption from the dominating Hindu zamindars, moneylenders and bureaucrats. But the Pakistan government was conscious of the unsurpassable distance between the Bengalis and the West Pakistanis in social matters, and a special linguistic and educational policy was created with this aim.

Three volumes on, *Purba Banglar Bhasha Andolon o Tatkalin Pajnity*, are pioneer works on the language movement; written by Badruddin Umar and published in 1970, they provide a thorough narrative description of the language movement in 1952. Umar admits that it is difficult for the Bangladeshis to view the language movement as something impersonal, since it is related to the sorrows and successes of the Bengali people.

The main source of government data was the contemporary Pakistan statistics department. Badruddin Umar in his books analyse the data, and these documents are the chief material for research on the language movement. In volume I, Umar briefly describes the initiation of the language movement, its primary manifestation as a language issue and eventually developing into a political struggle. He has also discussed the policies of the Muslim League and the Communist party.

Since the creation of Pakistan in 1947, there was actually no political organization, except for these two political parties. And the class character of these two parties, the theoretical and organizational line followed by them, their programmes and defects—all these placed the politics in East Bengal on a new, democratic platform. Centering all these, different political parties and class organizations grew up in East Bengal, by placing Muslim League at one end and the Communist party at the other.

The object of The Bengal Agricultural Debtors Act was to give provisions for scaling down debt of the agriculturists and deferring payment of the dues so scaled down, to the extent demanded by the inability of the debtors. In India two different methods have been tried for scaling down of debts, e.g., voluntary and compulsory.

In the first three chapters of the second volume, Badruddin Umar deals with the economic malady that had engulfed the East Bengal peasantry and describes the condition of the Bengal peasants in the twentieth century. The price of food crops, specially rice, increased in Bangladesh from the beginning of 1947 and the East Bengal government introduced the system of levies on the proprietors of the surplus land areas, with the aim of increase of revenue. It was decided that, the government would purchase surplus paddy at a definite price from the peasants and other proprietors of land, and the specific price fixed by the government was much lower than the standard market-price. This meant really a standardization of the levy. This and other factors decided the saleable amount of crops without taking note of the real amount of family surplus. The peasants were deprived of any economic benefit out of the policy followed by the central government, and went with a meager amount of food. For this reason, the peasantry in different regions of East Pakistan became rebellious against the bureaucrats who implemented the levy system.

Different reports were published in the newspapers in East Pakistan about the imposition of levies and generally the government's policy towards food collection. In this situation, the East Bengal government announced in the newspapers its decision to keep the food policy unchanged. Here Umar refers to the situation in August 1947, that is, the transfer of power to East Pakistan and alleges that, different groups warned the East Bengal as also the Pakistan government that the food situation may result in famines. However, the government did not take adequate steps to control the famine situation. After 14 August 1947, the food problem in East Pakistan became more acute and in the end the crisis resulted in famine.

Three types of causes led to the outbreak of famine, for which, the decaying, feudalistic system in Bangladesh may be the first factor; flood, heavy and low rainfall, problems related to water control were the second; thirdly, government policy and administrative corruption had its own contribution.

Badruddin Umar points out that the lack of contact was a great handicap for relief measures. The separation from the people was a very important reason for the failure of the famine resistance system, says Badruddin Umar. Before the 'Zamindari Purchase and Tenancy Act' was passed in 1950, due to the long-term peasant movements, the zamindars had been forced to reduce the exploitation of the peasants. But after the government acquired the zamindaris, the government and its employees began their extortion and exploitation in a new form. Previously, the peasants were not exempted from taxation, but they were usually allowed some time-span to gather money for tax-payment. They had personal relations with the zamindars or could form into regional pressure groups, and the zamindars were aware of that. But the situation as it stood in 1947, i.e., the peasants were deprived of that chance. Now it was found that tax collection started mechanically, body warrants for the peasants in case of delay in payment were issued, forcible occupation of the cattle became a regular practice and government employees like zamindari counterparts were in the habit of taking bribes. To get exemption from this kind of extortion, the peasants started taking loans from the merchants at higher rates. As a result, the land passed in the hands of the merchants from peasants. Umar says that this was more-or-less the overall condition of the peasants in East Bengal after the so-called abolition of the zamindari system.

In an analysis of the movement in the fifteenth chapter of the third volume, Badruddin Umar argues that the people in contemporary East Bengal took some time to realize the role of the central government in Pakistani administration. Their opinion in the first phase was that, some non-Bengali bureaucrats and Muslim League leaders outside the province were mainly responsible for the exploitation and extortion in East Bengal.

In conclusion, Badruddin Umar describes Pakistan as a new colony, and a field for imperialism, and the country acted as the agent of British American bloc. Hence, all kinds of popular extortions—be it economic, political and cultural—was related to imperialism, and the extortion and exploitation on the people of East Pakistan, were accounted for by the powerful imperialism existing in Pakistan.

The contemporary East Pakistan Communist Party, better known as the East Pakistan Organisation Committee of the Pakistan Communist Party, during the 1952 language movement, published a series of articles in different pamphlets and internal party circulars. The Communist party certainly grasped the imperialistic tendencies of the Pakistan government.

Badruddin Umar was the first scholar who placed the history of the language movement within the framework of socio-economic analysis. He has written a detailed history of how after the creation of Pakistan, the powerful central and regional leadership of the Muslim League adopted an autocratic policy in statecraft. But simultaneously, the democratic forces in East Pakistan gradually elaborated their movements. Badruddin Umar has processed a large amount of data in his three volume work in a magnificent way, and has also analysed how different classes in contemporary society grew rebellious towards the state. Badruddin Umar offers a detailed description of the consolidation of the democratic forces in the country vis-à-vis autocracy of the Muslim League. He shows, how a leadership alternative to that of the Muslim League was created and new organizations were established by them. It was this leadership that ultimately emerged victorious in East Pakistan's struggle for democracy. Badruddin Umar puts emphasis on the role of the political leadership and the educated middle class in this movement. He also marks how the other classes in society, like the peasantry, became united against Pakistan's oppression.

The next series on the language movement is, *Bhasha Andolon Patabhumi Granthamala*, and general editor Atiur Rahman is in search of, "The socio-economic background of the language movement". Atiur Rehman and Lenin Azad started a preliminary survey on the subject and the results of the project were divided into five volumes: 1. *Bhasha Andolon Pariprekhit o Bichar*, 2. *Bhasha Andolon Arthonoitik Patabhumi*, 3. *Bhasha Andolon o Rajnaitik Prabonotasomuho*, 4. *Bhasha Andolon Angshogrohonkarider Sreni Abasthan*, 5. *Bhasha Andolon Shahitwik Patabhumi*.

Rehman Sobhan in his preface to the first volume argues that, it is a historical truth that the majority of population in East Pakistan who had worked for the Pakistan movement before independence, were utterly disappointed and disillusioned once Pakistan was born. They were frustrated with the ruling coterie in Pakistan, and after the mother-language was attacked, the Bengalees became quickly separated from Pakistani nationalism. A kind of active conflict developed in the society of East Bengal, among different classes of people. The newly budding Bengali middle class crossed a phase of disappointment and uncertainties.

After the language movement, many people realized that the seeds of the revolt had been implanted within the middle class from the days of the past. The Muslim middle class had either participated in the movement or had supported it. But a feature that added to the complexity of the situation was that, most of the contemporary superior classes in East Bengal were Hindus, either zamindars, business men and professionals, and the support of the Muslims to the creation of Pakistan came due to the fact that they wanted to be economically free and prosperous, shaking off the subordination of the Hindu affluent classes. Therefore, the nationalist movement in East Pakistan was for gaining economic freedom. But their hopes were frustrated when they found that there was little chance of the development of the Bengali middle class within the Pakistani state-structure, which appropriated all power, and therefore the Bengali Muslims began to develop a kind of Bengali nationalism.

In the introduction to the first volume written by Atiur Rehman and Lenin Azad, there is noticeable difference between the self-interest of the ruling and that of the middle class in East Bengal. Historian Badruddin Umar accepts this theory, as also other researchers, and they believe that the language movement is to be understood in the context of the social, political and economic deprivation and extortion, which ultimately made the language movement a nationalist issue.

Incidentally, in this volume, Rehman and Azad added a critique on the ideas of different writers on nationalism, such as, Tom Nairn (*The Breakup of Britain*, 1977) or Eric Hobsbawm ('Some Reflections on *The Breakup of Britain*', New Left Review, No. 105). Here although different aspects of the concept of modern 'state' have been illuminated in different countries of the world, most of the regions have imperialism or neo-imperialism imposed on them. As a result, there was a great deficit of organizational elements within the state.

But he himself did not bring within his discussion the general participation of the ordinary people in the Pakistan movement, and therefore did not face the questions of how the population of a newly emancipated nation became so quickly involved in such a secessionist movement and how their national consciousness developed. He has surveyed the big problem mainly on the basis of difference of language between the two parts of the country.

Actually, further research has shown that, there was greater exploitation and extortion in the colonial period than the extortion described by Badruddin Umar, both before and after the language movement. Further, a definite reply to the question as to why such a huge movement happened in 1952 cannot be found in Badruddin Umar's writings. He has more or less ignored the question of leadership which led the movement to such a magnitude and Badruddin Umar's huge work is an important but only partial view of the history of the popular movement in East Bengal.

Certain questions have remained unanswered in this context, such as, which types of economic groups of families came out for leadership, whether rural or urban groups were stronger in the movement, what the idealism that led them to give leadership was and whether they could see the discrepancy at the time of the birth of Pakistan.

In the *Bhasha Andolon*: *Arthonoitik Patabhumi*, the authors, Atiur Rehman and Lenin Azad, paid attention to the economic situation in the pre-colonial period. In 1947, the state of Pakistan emerged as geographically separated into two parts and due to discrepancy in development planning, the standard of living of the general population in East Bengal deteriorated. Frequent famines, peasant rebellion, workers' dissatisfaction and strikes showed very poor living condition of the east Bengal population. As a result, the ordinary people as also the well-off middle class in East Bengal, separated from mainstream politics, were disappointed very quickly. The authors further point out that in the last phase of British rule, the major portion of the Indian industrialists belonged to the Hindu community, and naturally a rivalry developed between the Muslim peasants and the Hindu industrialists, businessmen and merchants, that is between the Hindu rich and the Muslim poor.

Just after the creation of Pakistan, the wealthy Sikhs and Hindus were largely driven out of west Pakistan, which led to the quick decline of population in towns of Pakistan. While most of the refugees who came to East Bengal were poor workers, they spread out in different parts of East Bengal in search of livelihood. Some of the industrialists of west Pakistan came to India with their capital, (now the newly formed state of Pakistan), there was no industrial town in East Bengal in '47; but in comparison in the eastern part there were big industrial towns like Calcutta, Jamshedpur, Bombay or Ahmedabad. The dividing force in Pakistan was a sense of false nationalism based on religion and its main aim was to bring out a portion named Pakistan from the clutches of the big Indian bourgeoisie. It was inevitable that the right of self-determination of a backward region like East Bengal would be deprived.

This complex situation, involving sectionalisation of industries, refugee problem, and poverty of the East Bengal Muslims, have been dealt with properly by Lenin and Azad, in contrast to Umar's work. Therefore, due to the partition of Bengal, a large number of jute, gold and other commodities went to India through the black market. It is noteworthy that, the large jute industry that had developed, depending on jute in East Bengal, fell in India's part, and consequently jute was sold in an illicit manner in India.

Before partition, Khulna, Jessore and Barishal were the chief supplier of food to Calcutta, while numerous jute mills of Calcutta helped to consume jute from East Bengal. But after partition, procurement and export of jute for Calcutta was controlled by west Pakistan, and East Pakistan where jute was grown was never given her dues. East Pakistan was the jute-producing country, but after partition, when there was a great demand for raw jute in the international market, and also for jute products, it was not the interest of the producer that the Pakistan government considered, but earned foreign exchange through jute-business.

The development planning adopted by the Pakistan government on the support of the capitalists and businessmen of West Pakistan reveals that there was a well-planned conspiracy for ruling East Pakistan through extortion. All the money earned from exports was mostly spent on Pakistan. The plans that were made to develop industries of government enterprise were all situated in West Pakistan. It seemed as if East Bengal was hardly a province of Pakistan.

In the concluding chapter of the second volume, Atiur Rahman and Lenin Azad discuss the inevitability of the revolt. It is a point to note that, Pakistan was born in 1947 through the partition of subcontinent. The peasant-population in East Bengal played a significant role in the Pakistan movement. Fazlul Huq and other leaders asked the peasants to participate in a political movement and the peasants responded positively due to their anti-feudal class-identity.

It is true that, the powerful Muslim League abolished the feudal system formally, immediately after the formation of Pakistan. But this was a reform only on paper. By that time, all the Hindu zamindars moved to West Bengal. And of course, a small Muslim intermediary class, who were beneficiaries of the zamindari system, faced some preliminary losses due to the decision of exchange of population but they were given enough compensation. Here also, wealth was necessary for development of the country, and agriculture would provide such wealth, while import of capital against goods sold, might provide another source of well being. East Bengal became a supplier of raw materials for that stagnant industry, and a type of 'internal colony' developed in East Bengal. The small number of peasants in west Pakistan were somewhat benefited from the industrial growth of west Pakistan, but the large agricultural base in East Pakistan suffered heavily, and emerged as an enclosed market.

In the third volume of the series, *Srenibhitti o Rajnaitik Prabanatasamuha*, M.M. Akash analyses the political trends in the pre-partition period. He states that in 1944, Abul Hashim took control of the Muslim League with a strong hand and published a manifesto on 24 March, 1945, on behalf of the Muslim League. The speech of this manifesto clearly reveals the contemporary political thoughts of the followers of Abul Hashim, who took control of the Muslim League with a strong hand and published a manifesto on 24 March, 1945, on behalf of the Muslim League. The speech of this manifesto clearly reveals the contemporary political thoughts of the followers of Abul Hashim, the contents of which had been described in Abul Hashim's autobiography.

H.S. Suhrawardy became the Chief Minister of Bengal after the elections and during his victory in the month of April, 1946, Jinnah called a convention of the members of the League of the Legislative Council in Delhi, in which Jinnah introduced the Lahore Bill and passed it, which planned for a United Pakistan consisting of East and West Pakistan. In analyzing the political ideas involved in the language movement, Akash narrated the nature of some elected organizations: 1. Tamaddun Majlish and Islamic fraternity, 2. Awami Muslim League, 3. Communist Party, 4. East Pakistan Youth League, 5. East Pakistan Students League and others. He further says that in totality, roughly three ideological tendencies in the Awami League can be detected: a. religious equality, b. petty bourgeois nationalism, c. liberal bourgeois democracy.

The twelve-point programme included the demand for regional self-rule under the federal state of Pakistan, for holding general elections in East Bengal, for recognizing Bengali as a state-language of Pakistan, for the nationalization of jute industry and abolition of the zamindari system without giving any compensation. In analyzing the role of the Communist Party, M.M. Akash states that the Congress was progressing with the plan of a pan-Indian state combining the provinces that lacked the right of self-determination and the Muslim League demanded the state of Pakistan, consisting of the majority of Muslim provinces in eastern and western India.

The biggest peasant struggle in Bengal in the end of 1946—which was known as the 'Tebhaga movement'—created an upheaval amongst the peasants of north, south and east Bengal, although, due to the communal environment, it failed to gain support from the middle and the working classes of the cities. But its firm base developed in the villages and this was how the Communist Party grew powerful in East Pakistan.

There were two features of the Bengali Muslim middle class: originated basically either from the aristocratic Nawab-zamindar group or from the surplus village peasant family. However, although the real origin of the Bengali Muslim middle class was of two types, later they combined the different sources of education-employment-profession into an ordinary group—which was named as the 'Bengali Muslim middle class'. It is noteworthy that in a later period when there started the presence of idealist tendencies and features of organized politics within the middle class, i.e., when this class gradually developed itself from a class-in-itself, then there was the reflection of the two distinctions earned from their birth.

The truth that comes out from the discussions in the second

chapter is that, however successful the pre-partition Muslim League was in unifying all the Muslim middle classes under its green banner, the task for enthusing the members in favour of partition had to be done by planting the seed. In reality, the unity of the contemporary period organized by the demand for Pakistan was only negative, i.e., the unity of the Muslims felt against the greater enemy, the Hindu upper and middle class. It was not that these inherent conflicts were in the Muslim League in an incipient form, even in pre-partition East Bengal. These conflicts were manifest through small party differences within the Muslim League. Some of such instances has been narrated by the author, and it comes out from the discussions that, the middle class related to the peasants in East Bengal combined in the first place under the leadership of Fazlul Huq of the Krishak Praja Party (1937), and created a democratic base against the Nazimuddin League that came under the supervision of the Nawab group. The picture of the modern liberal Sahid Suhrawardy who was standing between the two adversaries has also been illustrated here.

The fourth volume in the series deals with *Angshogrohonkarider Sreni Abasthan* and has been written by Atiur Rehman and Sayed Hashmi. The 'Forward' of the chapter says that, the people became disillusioned due to economic and other forms of crisis. The people of East Bengal became disappointed very quickly when they saw that in actual practices development of the material and cultural needs, for which they supported the demand for Pakistan, would not be fulfilled. And once there came an attack on the language of people of East Bengal, the progressive group of people became disappointed about the ruling class. They were educated, young and thoughtful. It was through their efforts that the ordinary people clearly understood the subordinate position of East Pakistan and the superiority of the Pakistani state.

In conclusion to the fourth volume, the authors elucidate fifteen points, which they regard as the truth and which they have derived by conducting sample-surveys of some leaders and participants in the language movement. The authors here lay stress on one particular point: the desire for materialistic and cultural development, which made the people of East Bengal participate in the Pakistan movement, had gradually evaporated. From the very first, they were isolated from the rulers and their supporters in the western part of Pakistan. When

Pakistan was established, the separation between the two was further increased by adoption of discriminatory economic and political policies by Pakistani rulers.

In spite of all these, the middle-class in East Bengal tried to survive within the political framework of Pakistan. Although they noted the bad symptoms of discrimination, they wanted to solve the problems within the Pakistani statistical framework through prayers and petitions in the first place, and then through democratic struggle.

A number of rejoinders have been given in the last part of this volume to illustrate this point. The first type deals with some case-studies, in which the role of a few involved in the language movement and interviews with them have been given. These include Abdul Matin, an important leader of the language movement, Justice Habibur Rahman Shelly, Oli Ahad, who was the General Secretary of the democratic Youth League of the contemporary period and many such others. The second kind of rejoinder dealt with the language movement outside Dhaka, and its extension to areas like Pabna, Kumilla, Chittagong, Bagura, Rajshahi, Sylhet, Jessore, Khulna, Barishal and other districts have been summarily dealt with in this section. There is much scope to elaborate this portion and the distinction between the character of the movement inside Dhaka and in the suburbs can be elucidated further.

The fifth volume in this series entitled, *Bhasha Andolon Shahitwik Patabhumi*, written by Humayun Azad deals with the intellectual background of the language movement. Azad in the foreword admits his responsibility to search for the social and cultural character of the Bengali literature between 1947 and 1951. It has been shown that, there was a great tendency of pro-Pakistanism in the different phases of literature in the period; and almost all the literateurs were trained in Pakistanism. In this phase, the common feature in the poems and articles was backwardness ("*progotiheenata*"). The magazines and newspapers were active in spreading Pakistanism and conservatism and they created a dark phase in Bengali literature.

The Pakistani theory of literature was socio-politically non-progressive, culturally backward and sterile. Its propagandists, who believed in the two-nation theory of the Muslim and Pakistani movements, were all criticized as reactionaries. They did not understand that Pakistan on which they had blind faith became brittle after independence; and they did not realize that the Bengalis have started to progress towards a new direction by ignoring Pakistan.

He shows how Pakistanism was propagated and rejected in poetry. It is said that the number of lyrical poems decreased, and comparisons became regular. Many poems were showing symptoms of real poetry. Azad gives a few illustrations from Shamsur Rahman and other poets and said that it became clear from the excerpts that the contents of these was different, and opposed to the enthusiasm of the Pakistani trends. Its word-selection and emotion was different. Such poetry tried to earn modernity—in subject and revelations; it was not oriented to the Middle East; with a flavour of a new feature of culture, not relevant to Pakistani literature.

According to Rajarshi Dasgupta, it is well-known that the apparent logic behind the partition, conceded as the cost of independence, was to apportion different states for Hindus and Muslims, in order to put an end to communal conflicts and riots witnessed in colonial India.[14] As would become evident from the paper, the developments in the subcontinent have clear links to the history of colonialism and the rise of ethnic nationalism on the one hand, and to the more recent American domination and its 'war on terror' on the other.[15] Particularly with regard to Muslim fundamentalism, there has been a clear escalation of the crisis since the Afganisthan campaign and the Gulf War, leading to the 9/11/ terrorist attacks.

If communalism is posing a formidable threat to 'underdeveloped' countries, then 'developed' nations must also cope with the challenge of 'multiculturalism' and migrant diaspora. Another relevant question in this regard is the relation of communalism to globalisation and the late-capitalist system. According to Dasgupta, this needs a separate study outside the scope of this paper.[16]

Notes

1. Jaya Chatterjee, *Bengal Divided*, p. 191.
2. Chatterji p. 266.
3. Ratanlal Chakrobarty, *Rural Indebtedness in Bengal.*
4. *Ibid.*, p. 1.
5. Ratanlal Chakrobarty, *Rural Indebtedness in Bengal*, p. 2.

6. *Ibid.*, p. 2.
7. *Ibid.*, p. 3.
8. *Ibid.*, p. 3.
9. *Ibid.*, p. 196.
10. *Ibid.*, p. 198.
11. *Ibid.*, p. 5.
12. *Ibid.*, p. 5.
13. *Ibid.*, p. 7.
14. Rajarshi Dasgupta, 'Representations of Communalism A Study of Recent Print media Reports in Bangladesh', Occasional Paper.
15. *Ibid.*, p. 3.
16. *Ibid.*, p. 3.

4

Islam and Islamic Fundamentalism in Bangladesh

The term "fundamentalism" came into vogue in the second decade of the twentieth century, with the publication of a series of pamphlets called, "The Fundamentals: A Testimony to the Truth", intended to serve as a resource for and defence of essential Christian doctrine, as was intended by those men who authored *The Fundamentals* and funded the work. It appeared between 1910 and 1915 through a set of conferences of the World's Christian Fundamentals Association in 1919. It was edited by A.C. Dixon and later by Reuben Archer Torrey in a set of 90 essays in 12 volumes published by the Bible Institute of Los Angels.

The articles presented in *The Fundamentals* were written as a response to the modernism and liberal theology of the latter part of the 19th century and beginning with the 20th. They were written in order to help missionaries, so that they might use the articles which would help them in affirming and reaffirming and explain the fundamental truths of Christianity in the face of ever increasing attacks against it. Those who funded the writing and publishing of the series did so at their own expense and all the books which were printed in the original twelve volume series were given free of charge as a service to the recipients. The pamphlets and books came out between 1910 and 1915 through a series of conferences, of the World's Christian Fundamentals' Association, held sometimes later.

Coming to the role of Islam in present-day Asian history, Professor Asim Roy is highlighting the nature and history of Islam in Bengal.[1] Roy argues that, the most fundamental form of external challenge to

Islam emanates from the twin pressures of westernization spreading through globalisation, as also a process of effective elimination of Communist threat to western capitalism in the wake of the break up of Soviet Union.[2] Incidentally, it should be noted that, the Islamic tradition dates its origin to events which unfolded in the early seventh century CE in the Arabian town of Mecca. The tradition teaches that a forty-year—old merchant, Muhammad ibn Abdallh—commonly referred to simply as the Prophet—or messenger, of God—receives a series of revelations from God beginning to 610 CE and ending soon before his death in 632 CE. These revelations, collectively known as the Quran, are held by Muslims to be God's direct and inalterable word and are the principal source of Islamic belief and practice.

The *Quran* and the *Hadith* are the two most important sources of Islamic religious and legal thought. Those with the task of interpreting the Quran and the Hadith are known as *ulama*, i.e., religious scholars. From their efforts emerged the code of regulations known as the Sharia, which in turn gave rise to Islamic law. Muslims acknowledge the Quran as the extension of the Divine into the earthly realm, the embodiment on earth of God's mercy, power and mystery.

According to Syed Anwar Hosain, although the concept of Islamic resurgence had its origin long ago, it became more prominent during the 1970s, and 'militant Islam' has been a kind of response to 'militant colonialism', 'militant Christianity', and 'militant secularism', imposed on Muslim countries through western expansionism of the nineteenth and twentieth centuries.[3] He says that, in the context of Bangladesh, the western instruction elicited three grades of responses: acculturationist, normative and neo-normative.[4] According to him, Sir Syed Ahmed Khan (1817-98) and Syed Amir Ali represented the acculturationist trend in British India.[5] Its impact, however, on present-day Bangladesh is only marginal. Syed Amir Ali (1849-1928), lawyer, spokesman on Indian Muslim concerns, and writer on Islamic history and society, was born on 6 April 1849 at Cuttack in Orissa. He was the fourth of the five sons of Syed Sadaat Ali, a descendant of a Shia family from Meshed in Iran. Ameer Ali's great-grandfather had migrated from Iran with the army of Nadir Shah in 1739, serving thereafter at the Mughal and Awadh courts. Soon after his birth his father, moved the family first to Calcutta, and then to Chinsura, where they upheld in modest comfort the lifestyle of the '*ashraf*' elite.

His family's origins strongly influenced Amir Ali's sense of own identity, leading to some criticism of him as alienated from the Bengali environment of his own childhood. Syed Amir Ali soon surpassed his brothers' educational attainments and prominence. Assisted by very close relationships with the British teachers at the Hooghly Maddrasa, and supported by several competitive scholarships, he achieved outstanding examination results, graduating from Calcutta University in 1867, and gaining the M.A. with Hons. in History in 1868.

He attributed to his mother a strong religious influence especially after his father's early death when Amir Ali was only seven yeas old. The family employed a resident '*moulavi*' who taught him the *Quran*, Arabic and Persian. Later he received more advanced tuition outside the home. A significant influence in the forming of his lifetime's interest in the origins, rise and nature of Islamic society was the nearby Hooghly *Imambara*.

Close to 20th century, Nawab Salimullah Khan got a clean slate for building up a conservative Muslim ideology. The history of Nawab Salimullah Khan of Dhaka has a particular role to play, in the evolution of the Muslim League in 1905. A special initiative was taken by the Dhaka Nawab family in the formation of a party for the Muslims.

Thus the initiative towards the creation of a separate Muslim homeland, though spurred by political rumblings from the days of Syed Ahmed Khan, had its own contextual and ideological specificity. It was the outcome of a political scenario on the eve of and during the Second World War that altered the political discourse in India and created, much to Jinnah's relief, the space for this maneuverings. A beleaguered government, which had in the past refused to deal with Jinnah, now turned to him for political and moral support and, in the process, legitimized his critique of the Congress claim to represent all the communities of India.

If Pakistan was still a pipe-dream, the Muslim League was little more than a paper organization. Having been in the wilderness during the agitation over the Khilafat, its membership had plummeted to 1,330 in 1927.[6] The 1929 session was adjourned for lack of quorum. When Iqbal presented his address in Allahabad in 1930, the meeting failed to muster the required quorum of 75 members.

The term neo-normative usually refers to those Muslim traditionalists who never waver in the theory of rejection of the western ideals as alien or ungodly to Islam. The Wahabi movement and the Faraizis stood for this type of Islam in British India, and carried militant movements against western rule. In present-day Bangladesh, the 'Jamaat-e-Islami', the 'Nezam-e-Islami' and the Khilafat movement are all champions of what has been described as normative Islam.[7]

The neo-normatives are consistent in affirming that Islam is the norm by which all reality should be measured and everyone judged. The most notable advocate of neo-normative Islam was Hasan al-Banna of Egypt who founded the Islamic brotherhood movement, and preached that Islam must be the main platform on which is built the past, present and the future of a country. It should be the guideline of public policy in a given state.

Islam is the third major monotheistic tradition to emerge in human history. The term *Islam* itself, often translated as "submission", refers to the decision by the Muslim ("One who submits or surrenders") to abide both in mind and body by the will of God.

The verses of the Quran were given to Muhammad, who in turn recited them to his followers. The word *Quran* itself means "recitation" and can refer to a part of the whole sacred text. According to the tradition, the Quran achieved its present, written form during the Caliphate of Uthaman, who ordered a group of respected Muslims to create a definitive version. It is composed of one hundred and fourteen chapters known as *sura*s, each of which bears both a number and a title, the latter usually a word or phase occurring early in the *sura*. While western scholars tend to cite Quranic chapters by number, Muslim writers generally refer to their title.[8]

The *sura*s are also identified as either "Meccan" or "Medinan", depending on whether they were revealed before or after the Hijra. The Meccan verses center on God's majesty and unity and the certainty that he is to bring his compassion and judgement to bear upon humanity and the world. In this context, Muhammad's role in the Meccan period, as he himself proclaimed, was to bring glad tidings of God's compassion, and to warn of the coming judgement that would separate the righteous from the wrongdoers.

The Meccan verses are often short, with intense imagery. But the Medinan verses contain similar ideas and languages, but reflect the new challenges facing Muhammad and the nascent Islamic community. The verses are generally longer and more complex and often express a concern for religious, moral and social order. More importantly, they describe the central duties of Islam: prayer, alms, fasting at Ramadan, and the pilgrimage to Mecca (the Haji). Quranic interpretation, or *tafsir*, forms part of the core of Islamic learning. All Muslims, therefore, bear the responsibility to see that a just and moral social order is created and maintained.

From early on in the development of legal tradition, the laws that govern Islamic life were perceived as essentially divided into two categories: those that concern the relationship between humankind and God; and those that relate to the intervention of the human community. In each of these spheres there are in turn five categories of human ethical behaviour. These acts are often referred to as the "Five Pillars" of Islam and constitute the Islamic ritual system. The Friday session of religion includes a sermon (*khutba*) delivered by a preacher, or prominent member of the community, and usually consists of commentary on a specific religious or social topic, and discussion of a specific Quranic verse or set of verses.

The chief difference between Shia and Sunni traditions is Shiism's belief in, and veneration of, a line of divinely inspired leaders known as Imams. This belief is grounded in a particular understanding of events in the early history of Islam. In his last address to his followers at Ghadir Khumm, Muhammad is said to have spoken of his son-in-law, Ali ibn Abi Talib.

Khomenian Iran, Palestanian Al-Hamas and Hizabullah, National Islamic Front of Sudan, Islamic Brotherhood of Egypt, Islamic revolutionaries in Algeria, Talibans and other Mujahideen in Afganisthan, Moros of the Phillipines, radical Muslims in Pakistan, Bangladesh, Indonesia, India and Malaysia, as also the sensitive Muslims in the western countries, as in the United States of America, United Kingdom and other European and Asian countries, are examples of radical Islamic power, and are objects of fierce curiosity and controversies of journalists and politicians. It shows that Islamic fundamentalism is at present a world-wide phenomenon, and is going to put its imprint on world-economy and politics. Fundamentalism in Bangladesh is only a chapter in this universal movement.

There is an extraordinary degree of vagueness and confusion

about what constitutes Islamic fundamentalism. Asim Roy admits that, serious problem with the meaning of "Islamic fundamentalism" does exist, as various Muslim social groups take advantage of the flexibility of the idea, in order to serve their own interests. Unfortunately, in most cases, fundamentalists are far away from the basic principles of the religion they claim to espouse. In reality the leading Islamic fundamentalists are mostly using Islam as a political tool rather than trying to return to the fundamentals of Islam. One such example may be Osama Bin Laden, who struck terror in the name of Islam. Taliban militancy is also a kind of political threat in Afganisthan and other parts of Asia. This has resulted in a widespread unrest among the masses of the Islamic world, who are now totally confused. The cries of suffering, anguish and anger arising from the continuing tragedy of vagueness of destination, the confusion about the goal to be achieved and the path to be followed, remain drowned under the ocean of arguments of the so-called resurgent Islam. The debates and discussions on the so-called fundamentalist Islam, both at popular and scholarly levels, have conduced to foster and create monolithic, but stereotyped and imaginary, concepts of Islam. As Edward Said points out, this is the fact of betrayal of Muslim masses by their elites, who cannot offer any solid structure or base ground for the masses to depend upon.

The Sunni fundamentalist Muslim society in Saudi Arabia supports monarchy and Shia fundamentalist society in Iran supports republicanism. Again, Gaddafi in Syria analyses himself as an Islamic socialist. All these leaders are not fundamentalists of one type. But certain features are common to them all—such as the absence of the right to give independent opinions, absence of freedom of speech, and the existence of a despotic state-power ruling over everything of course. These characteristics are to be found in all fundamentalist societies and states—both Islamic and non-Islamic. These 'fundamentalists' do not believe in democracy, and fundamentalism has emerged as a threat to orderly growth of arts and culture, history and civilization in many parts of the world. It is now an established fact that, fundamentalism is a danger to order and stability, life and liberty, and to government leaders in Egypt, Algeria, Tunisia, Jordan, Saudi Arabia and other Gulf countries too.

1947-52, the Period of Initial Problems of New Nation-Building in a Colonial Framework

An analysis of events in East Pakistan between 1947 and 1971 reveals in the first place, economic and political discrimination against East Pakistanis, and secondly, snapping the communal bond of Islam that had been constructed between the people of various parts of Pakistan. 1947-52 were, for East Pakistan, the upcoming of the initial problems of new nation-building in a subordinate framework. Along with the various political and economic problems that the newly born Pakistan had to face, two important issues were gradually driving a wedge between the East and west part of Pakistan. The first question that made the two parts of the nation slowly moving apart, was the language issue; the second, economic extortion by West Pakistan of the territory standing on the east, i.e., East Pakistan. At this stage, an overview of the language problem (leading to the language movement in East Pakistan) may be attempted, the economic and political problems to be dealt with later. It should be borne in mind that it was the emergence of linguistic nationalism that was the prima facie factor behind the birth of Bangladesh.

Islamization of East Pakistan and Arabicization of the Bengali language and literature, ignited that language movement of 1952. Whereas the Urdu-speaking elite of West Pakistan was greatly influenced by western trends taking a new colour in the 1930s, with a written language using Arabic script, East Pakistan was culturally homogenous with West Bengal in India. With West Bengal it shared a long common history, a rich cultural heritage and a sanskrit-like script. This was one of the fundamental differences between the East and West of the newly born state of Pakistan, which led eventually to the emotional upsurge for gaining priority of the Bengali language. The language movement took a radical turn in the 1950s, leading to widespread student discontent and slaughter of several Bengali students in East Pakistan. It is to be considered whether the seeds of separatism were sown in this movement.

Initial Politics of Communalism and Regionalism

Pakistan was the product of, among many other things, a national movement among the Muslims of British Indian empire. The all-Indian national movement, which failed to give adequate recognition to the special feelings or requirements of Indian Muslims, probably brought out a reaction among the Muslims for separatist tendencies. However, it is far from clear whether a separate territorial state is what even the Muslim League had in mind until very late, or, could have insisted on, but for the irreconcilable bent of mind of Jinnah. Eric Hobsbawm is certain that the bulk of ordinary Muslims thought in communal and not in national terms, and would not have understood the concept of national self-determination. To them any idealistic concept was something that would apply only to faith in Allah and his Prophet in East Pakistan, the movements of protest acquired communal, ethnic and linguistic character, all varied from each other, and finally became a national movement.[9]

A note may be added in this context on the proposal given by Abul Hashim, the Secretary of the Bengal Provincial Muslim League, dated 23 May 1947, who pointed out that, free Pakistan states should be governed and administered by the will and consent of the entire people, on the basis of universal adult suffrage. At the same time Abul Hashim has given in some detail a plan for a United Bengal which he and Sri Sarat Bose had prepared on 20th May, in the house of the latter.[10] The text of this United Bengal scheme is documented in *Bangladesher Swadhinata Yuddha Dalilpatra* and gives in some details the structural framework. To quote from it, "The following is the text of the tentative agreement signed by Sarat Chandra Bose and myself (Abul Hashim): 1. Bengal will be a free state. The free state of Bengal will decide its relations with the rest of India; 2.... election to the legislature on the basis of joint and adult franchise".[11] This draft was sent by Sri Sarat Bose to Mohandas Karamchand Gandhi for approval, with the expectation that if the Congress and Muslim League members of Bengal agreed to the proposal and signed a treaty. Jinnah himself might accept it without a fuss. Gandhi himself considered Bose and Hasim's proposal seriously, emphasizing that the province of Bengal has a very rich cultural tradition, and the mother tongue of all in the province is Bengali.[12]

Gandhi, in a letter to Sarat Chandra Bose on June 8, 1947, wrote, "I have now discussed the scheme roughly with Pandit Nehru and Sardar. Both of them were dead against the proposal and they are of the opinion that it is merely a trick for dividing Hindus and Scheduled Caste leaders.[13] It seems therefore that giving Bengal a separate identity, and making it a nation, was an idea that had been already found a place among the leaders of pre-partition era. The voice of protest was already there.

Mohammed Ali Jinnah's vision of a Pakistan free from communal cleavages found expression in some of his speeches. In his inaugural address to the Constituent Assembly of Pakistan on 11 August, 1947, in his capacity as its first President, he called upon the people to make progress by changing their past and working together in a spirit that everyone, no matter to what community he belonged, was first and foremost a citizen of the state of Pakistan.[14] He said, "...We should work together in the spirit and in course of time, all these angularities of the majority and minority communities—the Hindu community, the Muslim community—Pathans, Punjabis, Shias, Sunnis and so on... Brahmins, Vaishnavis, Khatris, also Bengalis and Madrasis—and so on—will vanish".[15] In his farewell message to East Pakistan on 28 March, 1948, he admitted that although East Bengal was an underdeveloped province, it possessed vast potentialities of raw materials and hydro-electric power. He hoped that given peaceful conditions and the fullest co-operation from all sections of the people, the province may be the most prosperous in Pakistan.[16] He congratulated the people that despite the persecution and massacre of Muslims in the months immediately following partition, he had seen the minority community going its normal avocation in perfect security.

Jinnah further said that, there had been disturbances in the Indian dominion, in which Muslims had been persecuted, and this in turn had given rise to fears in the mind of the minority community that unpleasant repercussions might occur in East Bengal. But such apprehension had been belied by actual facts. Moreover, he found that the provincial government had always taken whatever steps possible for the protection and well-being of the minority community and had done their best to dissuade them from leaving their ancestral home in East Bengal for an unknown fate in the Indian Union. He announced that there would be absolute freedom of the people to go to temples, mosques or to any other place of worship in the state of Pakistan. He assured that in the days of the future there would be no discrimination between one community and another; no discrimination between one caste or creed and another. In other words, the nationality Jinnah visualized was Pakistan, not just Muslims.

The Islamic ideology, on which Jinnah had based Pakistan, began to fade away, and regional feeling grew fast in East Bengal. Regionalism was the "raison d' etre" for the emergence of Bangladesh. General G.W. Chowdhury, who used to believe in one Pakistan, maintained that the most serious challenge[17] to Pakistani nationalism was economic disparity between East and West Pakistan. Many moderate East Pakistani leaders, like Nurul Amin and others who wanted to live in a united Pakistan, strongly urged the government to accelerate the economic development of East Pakistan and thereby remove the most serious grievance of the Bengali separatists. But unfortunately no one listened carefully or seriously to this advice. Political power was exercised by a narrow oligarchy which looked at the whole situation entirely from a new angle of maintaining "law and order" and it was futile to expect any imaginative economic programme or plans.

On the other hand, a different viewpoint comes out from the contemporary speech of Ghyasuddin Pathan. In a general discussion on the General Budget in the Constituent Assembly of Pakistan (1948), Ghyasuddin Pathan pointed out that in pre-British history of India the Bengalis were portrayed as a martial race who had won in many battlefields.[18] It was due to the mischievous policy of the British rulers that the raising of the army from amongst the Bengalis was stopped and in the freedom movement Bengal was the first amongst other Indian provinces to plunge itself into the fight. This was one of the reasons for depriving the Bengalis from the right of participating in the army. Pathan stressed that with the achievement of independence of Pakistan, the old outlook of the masters should be changed and thus he differed from Chowdhury who maintained that the breakup of Pakistan was due to bad handling of administrative problems. Thus it seems that, Jinnah realized clearly that if Pakistan was to exist as a modern state, its basis must be secular.[19] But Jinnah's death in September 1948 halted the trend towards secularism and his successors proved themselves unequal to the task of tackling the various problems facing the new-born state.

The history of United Pakistan from 1947 to 1971 is one of constant conflict between Pakistani nationalism, which could acquire a definite identity, and the emerging Bengali regionalism or sub-nationalism. In this connection, the opinion of General

G.W. Chowdhury may be relevant. According to G.W. Chowdhury, the Hindu-Muslim differences that gave rise to Muslim nationalism in India had six hundred years of history behind it, and were the product of "fundamental factors".[20] He argues that Jinnah based his demand for a separate state for the Muslims on the principle of the right of self-determination, and that no serious observer of the Indian political scene before independence could challenge the grounds on which he based his two-nation theory. Ultimately both the British government and the Indian Congress led by Gandhi and Nehru were forced to accept his pleas, and the partition of 1947 was the result of an agreement among British authorities, the Hindus and Muslims.[21]

The Bengali sub-nationalism or regionalism was, in the viewpoint of Chowdhury, "the product of a number of unfortunate or accidental factors connected with internal political developments in Pakistan in the 1950s and 1960s, particularly after the eclipse of the democratic process of the country which denied the Bengalis their due share in the political process."[22] Chowdhury points out that, at the time of independence of Bangladesh the Indian civil service left behind by the British 'raj' contained only one Bengali officer.[23] Similarly, the Bengalis were very poorly represented in the Army because the British authorities considered them a non-martial race, and there were "therefore some historical reasons for the preponderance of West Pakistani civil and military officers in East Bengal".[24] But after independence nothing was done to rectify the situation and, in the absence of a genuine democracy, with the country run by an oligarchy of civil and military officials, the Bengalis found themselves in the position of a colonial people.

Pathan points out that seamen from East Bengal had entered every water on the globe, and had received the appreciation and administration of foreign admirals.[25] It was, therefore, incumbent upon the government to provide facilities quickly to the people of East Bengal for naval training and to develop Chittagong as a center. Regarding recruitment in the airforce, East Bengal was being treated in a stepmotherly way and there were six or seven recruiting centers in West Pakistan whereas there was only one in East Pakistan. Pathan argued that since East Pakistan was physically separated, it should be regarded as a separate physical unit, and defence and development should be made on equal proportion in the eastern and western zones of Pakistan state. He appealed to the Assembly to make East Bengal self-sufficient in every respect.

On the side of Pakistan, Jinnah came out with a speech at a public meeting at Dhaka on March 21, 1948, where he said, he was conscious of a feeling in certain parts of the province against non-Bengali Muslims, and excitement prevailed over the question whether Bengali/ Urdu should be the state-language of Pakistan. Within a few days, in a speech at Dhaka University Convocation on 24 March, 1948, he further explained on students role in nation-building, and offered the people of the province a choice by using any language they wish for official use.[26] However, the language for inter-communication between the various provinces of the state should be Urdu, a language nurtured by a hundred million Muslims of the sub-continent, understood throughout the length and breadth of Pakistan and embodied the best that was in Islamic culture and Muslim tradition. Also, it was nearest to the language used in other Islamic countries. In his opinion, if the competent parts of the state were to march forward in unison, the language used could only be Urdu. In subsequent years, in the post-Mujib period, even in independent Bangladesh the trend to develop fraternal relation with Islamic countries of the Middle East, and also, financial dependence on them became quite apparent. It seems that this feature of the state-policy of Bangladesh had its deep root in the past, in the East Pakistanis led by Mohammed Ali Jinnah.

Notes

1. Asim Roy, *Islam in South Asia A Regional Perspective*, p. 1 (South Asian Publishers, New Delhi).
2. *Ibid.*, p. 1.
3. Syed Anwar Hosain, 'Islamic Fundamentalism in Bangladesh' Internal Variables and External Inputs' in Rafiuddin Ahmed edited, Religion, Nationalism and Politics in Bangladesh p. 138 (South Asian Publishers, New Delhi).
4. *Ibid.*, p. 139.
5. *Ibid.*, p. 139.
6. Mushirul Hasan, *India's Partition*, p. 1.
7. *Op. cit.*, p. 140.
8. Michael D. Coogan *World Religions: The Illustrated Guide*, p. 104.

9. Eric Hobsbawm, *Nations and Nationalism Since 1780 Programme, Myth, Reality*, p. 70 (Cambridge, 1993) "It is by no means evident that Pakistan was the product of a national movement among the Muslims of the then Indian empire, though it may well be regarded as a reaction against an all-Indian national movement which failed to give adequate recognition to the special feelings of or requirements of Muslims, and though, in an era of the nation-state, territorial partition seemed to be the only available formula, it is far from clear that a separate territorial state is even what the Muslim League had in mind until very late, or would have insisted on but for the intransigence of Jinnah..."
10. Abul Hasim *Amar Dekha Rajnitir Panchash Bchar*, p. 133.
11. *BSJD*, Volume 1.
12. Hashim, p. 136. *op. cit.*
13. Abul Hasim, *In Retrospection*, p. 158.
14. Quaid e-Azam Mohammad Ali Jinnah *Speeches as Governor General of Pakistan*, 11August 1947.
15. Quaid-e-Azam Mohammed Ali Jinnah: *Speeches as Governor General of Pakistan 1947-8*, p. 6.
16. *Ibid.*, p. 107.
17. G.W. Chowdhury, *The Last Days of United Pakistan*, p. 8.
18. Constituent Assembly (Legislature of Pakistan) Debates volume 1 of 1948 (1st March, 1948).
19. Moudud Ahmed Bangladesh: *Constitutional Quest for Autonomy.*
20. G.W. Chowdhury, *The Last Days of United Pakistan* (p. 3, UPL, 1994).
21. *Ibid.*, p. 3.
22. *Ibid.*, p. 3-4.
23. *Ibid.*, p. 6.
24. G.W. Chowdhury, p. 7.
25. Constituent Assembly (Legislature of Pakistan) Debates Volume 1 of 1948 (1st March).
26. Quaid-e-Azam Mohammed Ali Jinnah *Speeches as Governor General of Pakistan*, Speech at Dhaka University Convocation on 24 March, 1948.

5

1947-71: Birth of a Nation

In 1871, Germany, the strongest power of modern Europe was born out of broken pieces of area in central Europe. Germany in Europe had the advantage of being set up as a homogenous political structure, which, by utilizing its resources, could reach the height of a world power, and expand in a multitudinous way.

Hundred years later, in Asia a new state of Bangladesh is born with all the expectation of holding a parallel position to India, expanding and strengthening itself on the roots and plants of Islamic structure. It was a break-away country from the western part lying far away, and unlike modern Germany, was not well-equipped with natural resources. Instead of one, India faced itself with two separate Islamic nations on her western and eastern side. The Punjabis and the Bengalis, while they are Muslims existing in Pakistan and Bangladesh, are still parts of a wider community. But instead of gaining a superior position in south Asia, the story of Bangladesh became a tale of repeated changes and fluctuations in the structure of its government and polity, which so far, up to this day, is entangled with its internal problems, and hardly capable of putting up a strong countenance.

At the outset, one can suggest that the problem of East Pakistan was two-fold. In the first place, since the emergence of Pakistan as an independent state, those who dominated the Central Government, remaining predominantly West Pakistani in composition (despite occasional changes up to the time of the military take-over in 1958), have consistently tried to impose (and greatly succeeded too) a cultural, economic and military hegemony upon East Pakistan.[1] The relative strength of cultural, economic and political motivations in this design may be a matter of debate.[2] The second problem that has rocked Bangladesh now and again, was the emergence of the shadow of fundamentalism (religious) that made the country unable to achieve a stable, liberal administration. Scholars agree that fundamentalism in Bangladesh is largely the result of the activities of one party—'Jamat-i-Islami', which was founded by Sayyid Abul-Ala-Mawdudi (1903-1979), on 26 August, 1941, at Lahore. After the foundation of the Pakistan state, Mawdudi left Pathancoat of East Punjab for Lahore, where he organized the 'Jamaat-i-Islami', with a view to the introduction of Islamic administrative system in his country. Since 1949 Mawdudi began to serially publish his six-volume work, *Tahfimal-I-Quran* and completed it in 1972. This book gradually penetrated into Islamic thought and was effective enough to stamp religious bigotry into the hearts of the people.

A chronological history of Pakistani administration: After the formation of Pakistan, the Bengali Muslims in East Pakistan, with their varied literature and culture, view of life and nationalist feeling based on language, tilted towards secularism in 1948. They realized the significance and importance of factors other than religion for the formation of society, community, nation and state. But the rulers of West and a part of Bengali Muslims in East Pakistan ignored this trend, so that cultural communalism and Islamic fundamentalism came to be nurtured by and large by the people of East Pakistan. The large-scale Hindu-Muslim riots in the 1950s, conspiracy to change the Bengali script, the introduction of military rule in the year 1958 by demolishing democracy—all these events had a big pressure in building East Pakistan's cultural and political dimensions. In both wings of the Pakistan state, the '*Jamaat-e-Islami*' organized a movement in support of its Eight Point Demand, which raised the slogan of an Islamic constitution. As in the Pakistan period, so in the period following a successful liberation struggle and the birth of independent Bangladesh, the ruling circle were trying to misuse religion and Islamic dogma in order to preserve their authority.

The history of the movements of protest of East Pakistan between 1947 and 1971 is well-chronicled, and there are a wide range of books that reveal how the Awami League, different factions of the National Awami Party and many other parties and groups clashed with each other and worked over distinct possibilities for gaining autonomy or independence.

The first clash: The Movements of Protest: The ideology of Islamic unity was employed by Pakistan early in the post-independence period to deny the validity of the claims and demands of the minority groups—the Bengalis, Sindhis, Pathans and Baluchis, for the recognition of their distinct identity and needs. The first signs of unrest in East Pakistan appeared only a few months after partition, and were provoked by the decision to impose Urdu as the official "national language" of Pakistan. The Hindu elite of the pre-1947 era was replaced by the Muslim elite mainly as a result of violence, which either destroyed or pushed out the members of the older elite into the neighbouring state of India.

In February 1948 agitation for Bengali language spread throughout East Pakistan, with students in the vanguard of the movement, supported by other sections of the Bengali society. The students set up an action committee, and elaborated a series of demands which, while being radical in the context of the existing political situation, were basically 'petit-bourgeois' demands in nature. Hamza Alavi suggests that through this movement, the agitators hoped to rise to senior positions in the bureaucracy or to enter the newly created business community in Bengal.

Large numbers of people left the Pakistan President M.A. Jinnah's meeting in Dhaka in March 1948 when he reaffirmed his policy that Urdu must be the only state-language and in many schools and colleges angry students removed Jinnah's portraits. In his convocation address at Dhaka University he repeated his earlier remarks, and the ensuing chaos made it impossible for him to finish his speech. At a later discussion with the Student Action Committee the atmosphere became heated, and the meeting ended in a stalemate. The movements of the Bengali students in East Pakistan had the first martyrs on 21 February, 1952, when the police opened fire on a protesting crowd, killing twenty-six persons and wounding four hundred others.

The census of 1951 showed that Urdu was the mother-tongue of only 2 million citizens in Pakistan, which constituted 3.3 per cent of total population, and that only 7.3 per cent could speak Urdu at all. Each province in West Pakistan spoke its own language, and in East Pakistan the language was Bengali. On the basis of census-figures alone Bengali should have been the national language of Pakistan. Tariq Ali comments that, "this was quite clearly a ludicrous idea".[3]

The protesters were marching in Dhaka in the cause of the Bengali language. On the occasion of the first anniversary of the 'Martyrs' Day', ('*Shahid Dibash*') prisoner Munir Chowdhury wrote the drama '*Kabar*', that was staged by the Communist state-prisoners in Dhaka Central Prison on 21 February, 1953.

Hamza Alavi points out that, although the focus of the movement was the issue of national language, close to the hearts of the students and the educated middle class, it was still instrumental in creating radical consciousness of Bengali nationalism that extended beyond the immediate interests of those student-leaders who voiced the slogans of the language movement and gave it leadership.[4] The educated Hindu intelligentsia of Dhaka University had mostly migrated to Calcutta at the time of partition, and the student community in Dhaka in the post-partition period consisted primarily of Muslims from rural Bengal, who came for higher studies in the first generation. They were less well-off than the urban elite and depended on agricultural production and the export of rural products (mainly jute), for the continuance and financing of the studies. This class of newly educated Muslims of East Pakistan was drawn overwhelmingly from the villages and maintained a close conflict with the village society, i.e., they still had links with the rural world. Under conditions of widespread public discontent, the problems and demands of the rural population impoverished first by the depression of the 1930s, then by the famine and war in the 1940s, influenced both the rank and file and the leaders of the movement. The aspirations were to get regional share in government jobs, especially with places for themselves in the bureaucratic establishment.

Hamza Alavi locates two trends in the Bengali language movement. In the first place, there was a petty-bourgeois elitist tradition for those who hoped to rise to senior positions in the bureaucracy or to become members of the newly-created business community in Bengal on the strength of governmental financial support and subsidy. Secondly, there was a rural populist tradition that articulated the frustrations and aspirations of the long-suffering sections of the peasantry. The two traditions were intertwined but remained distinct, since the educated sons of the rich peasants had other aspirations than those of the peasantry in general.

At the vanguard of the Bengali language movement in the early

1950s was the Awami League Party. The foundation of the Awami League, the first Muslim opposition party in East Bengal, brought many dissatisfied factions on one platform. Soon the Awami League became the chief spokesman of the budding vernacular elite. An examination of the Awami League's leadership reveals some of the characteristics of the Bengali counter elite. The party president, Maulana Abul Hamid Khan Bhasani, was a peasant leader, a former President of the Assam Muslim League, a *maulana* with little formal education, who had a long record of political imprisonment. Maulana Bhasani was the only political leader in Pakistan who had attempted, though with limited success, to build a rural base of support in East Pakistan. The three vice-presidents—Abul Mansur Ahmed, Ataur Rahman Khan and Abdus Samad Khan—were all small-town lawyers with little active political experience. The General Secretary, Shamsul Huq, was a young student leader who came to prominence during the 1948 language demonstrations. The assistant General Secretary, Sheikh Mujibur Rehman, was another young student leader who came to light during the 1948 movement. Thus the Awami League's leadership was dominated by *mofussil* lawyers and students—vernacular potential professionals.

The Awami League provided a political organization for raising the vernacular elite, but they still lacked a coherent platform. Early Awami League demands and demonstrations dealt with issues such as food shortages and the restoration of civil liberties.

Another group which attempted to start democratic movement in Bengal, was the *Ganatantric Dal* (GD) founded in 1953 by a group of radical intellectuals and Communists. Under the Presidency of Haji Mohammed Danesh, a veteran peasant-movement leader and his associate Mohammad Ali, the party's General Secretary, the GD displayed rare unity and discipline. The GD platform called for the establishment of a democratic federal Republic of Pakistan with guarantee of full autonomy and equality for East Bengal, abolition of feudalism, industrialization, and dissociation of Pakistan from the British Commonwealth and a foreign policy of neutralism. With the secularization of the Awami League in the mid-1950s, and the change of name from Awami Muslim League to Awami League, the *Ganatantric Dal* faded rapidly from Pakistan's political scene.

At the head of the "elitist faction" of the Awami League was

Hosain Shaheed Suhrawardy, ex-Chief Minister of Bengal. He admits that he differed from the policy of the Pakistan government on certain fundamental issues and found himself in the opposition party. In his opinion, the government should give firm assurances to the minorities and should encourage them to stay and look after their safety and welfare instead of regarding them with suspicion and distrust and alarming them by charging them with disloyalty. According to him they had every right to be treated on a par with the Muslims as integral nationals of Pakistan. Such a policy would contribute substantially to the safety of the Muslims of India. Secondly, he was opposed to the theory of Liaquat Ali Khan that the Muslim League should be the one and only political party in the country for Muslims and that any Muslim who opposed it, or opposed the policies of his Muslim League government, was a traitor to the state.

Hence an attempt was lodged to victimize Suhrawardy. A law was passed in 1948 under which a member who had not become a permanent resident of Pakistan and resided there for about six months could lose his membership if the speaker of the House so desired. No nationality law had been passed until then.

So long as the Quaid-E-Azam, who was also the speaker of the Constituent Assembly, was alive, no seats were taken to unseat Suhrawardy. But after his death and no sooner Suhrawardy publicly declared that he was definitely planning to settle permanently in West Pakistan on and from 5 March 1949, than Liaquat Ali Khan induced the Speaker, Moulovi Tamizuddin Khan, to terminate his membership in the Constituent Assembly on 26 February 1949.

Sheikh Mujibur Rehman who was a protégée of Suhrawardy and schooled by him in politics, had political commitments firmly with him. On the other hand, Hamza Alavi argues that there was also a "populist" tradition in the Awami League, which flourished under the leadership of Maulana Bhasani. While the elitist leadership of Suhrawardy was largely concentrated in towns and cities, the populists had large number of cadres in the field in villages. Since the Communist Party was illegal, quite a number of Marxists joined the Awami League, so that it had a solid core of Marxists as well.

The left-oriented Krishak Sramik Party (KSP) of the veteran octogenarian, Suhrawardy's predecessor as ex-Premier of Bengal, A.K. Fazlul Haque, joined forces with the Awami League and the

Students League, to link the Bengali language with the wider political issue of autonomy.

A United Front comprising the Awami League, the KSP, the Nizam-I-Islami and the *Ganatantric Dal* was formed in 1953; and a common election manifesto, the 21-Point formula, was drawn up. This United Front and its 21-point manifesto foreshadowed later political trends in East Pakistan. The United Front was the first of a series of coalitions. United more against the Muslim League than for any positive policy, it consisted of various antagonistic forces, among which factionalism was rife from the start. According to Rounaq Jahan, East Pakistani politics had been dominated by political movements which aim more at getting power than at achieving specific policies. The coalition manifesto comprised a number of conflicting goals. Still it was a significant document, in so far as it was accepted by all the opposition groups and it contained the salient points on which a consensus was reached by the Bengali counter elite. The major thrust of the 21 point manifesto was the accommodation of the vernacular elite's interests. Twelve of the points expressed their demands.

While the 21 Points were essentially a programme for the vernacular elite, they also included demands directed toward mobilizing support from workers and peasants. Thus it called for the introduction of economic and social rights for the industrial workers, according to the principles of the International Labour Organisation.

The strategy proved a success. The Muslim League was swept out of office, and the vernacular elite came to power. Their party, the United Front, was able to administer a major defeat on the Muslim League in the East Pakistan State Assembly elections of 1954.

By May 1954, the Awami League-KSP agitators had won their major linguistic demand when the central government recognized the constitutional equality of Bengali with Urdu as a national language. It has been pointed out that the Bengalis, for their part, unlike the non Urdu-speaking West Pakistanis never really made a serious attempt to learn Urdu as a second language. It is significant, too, that after the 1954 elections, the East Pakistan Communist Party was banned and remained underground throughout the rest of the period during which East Bengal continued to be a part of Pakistan. In the 1954 elections, twenty-two communist candidates sponsored by the

United Front had won seats. The Fazlul Haque ministry as formed in 1954 was dismissed within a few days of taking office, on 29 May, 1954, by the Pakistan government, headed by Liaquat Ali Khan.

Therefore, the 1954-6 period, during which Suhrawardy was drawn into the "central" or western arena, witnessed a temporary but noticeable cooling down of Bengali linguistic nationalist ardour.

In the context of what happened in East Pakistan in 1954, an attempt may here be made to analyse the character of the group who stood for the language movement in the '50s and '60s. Tazeen M. Murshid[5] elaborates Rounaq Jahan's model when she points out that the vernacular intelligentsia failed to compel their opponents to arrive at a political understanding despite the numerical strength of their supporters which mainly was due to the fact that the central government was ruling through the army, on which the East Pakistani agitators did not have a shadow of influence. In fact, the tendency to opposition among the vernacular intelligentsia, slight in the 40s and 50s, became assertive and violent in the late 60s.

According to Murshid, although the intelligentsia may not be strictly occupation-related, certain occupations tend to be associated with it because of their intellectual response of the world. Tazeen Murshid assumes that the majority of the non-Muslim intelligentsia was Hindu for it comprised the majority of the non-Muslims and also educationally the most advanced.

Quoting from M.A. Rahim, *The History of Dhaka University* (Dhaka, 1987), Murshid claims that, while Muslims provided the bulk of teachers and professors, a large proportion of senior posts in higher education were filled by the non-Muslims. Tazeen Murshid points out that, in the years following partition, the proportion of non-Muslims in the middle class and amongst the intelligentsia decreased, while that of Muslims increased.

Taking education as a criterion for defining the intelligentsia, Murshid notes that it was possible to enter the ranks of the educated people with minimal education in the 50s and the 60s. Tazeen Murshid in her book makes an attempt to trace the socio-economic base of the intelligentsia and since university students are included in the category defined as intelligentsia, the analysis is based on available surveys on the living and working conditions of the educated community.

Murshid points out that the new middle class came now largely from the peasantry. Early intellectuals of both the pre-and post-1947 periods came from an established structure of old society with strong links with big landowners, propertied families or civil servants and professionals. She further gives the opinion that the stronger rural base of intellectuals in the later phase as revealed by recruitment patterns into East Bengal universities, indicates an increased degree of social mobility in the 60s and 70s, as compared to the 40s and the 50s. Tazeen Murshid therefore concludes that the Muslim intelligentsia which continued to emerge in East Bengal after partition could be describable as rural and vernacular not only because of their origin but also because the language they came to accept as their own, Bengali. This group was quite different in their outlook from the upper '*asraf*' people. Murshid argues that, the vernacular intelligentsia was the most vocal in trying to find the rightful place for Bengalis—socially, politically and culturally. In the process, it came to challenge the traditional patterns of authority embedded in the non-vernacular '*ashraf*' intelligentsia, which formed the power elite in the immediate post-partition period.

This latter group comprised the Urdu-speaking upper class of Bengal, and migrants from Punjab and Muslim minority provinces of India. Due to the origin of a large section of the intelligentsia in provinces other than Bengal, such as Uttar Pradesh and Bihar, their mother tongue was not Bengali and they tended to be of '*asraf*' descent—Liaquat Ali Khan, the first Prime Minister of Bengal, is a prime example.

Murshid admits that the vernacular and non-vernacular intelligentsia was not ideologically homogenous or closed groups. Some among the non-vernacular intelligentsia supported the vernacular ones: Azam Khan, for example, who was the governor of Pakistan, represented such a counter-tendency. Among the vernacular intelligentsia were people like Monem Khan, also a governor of East Pakistan, Professor Syed Sajjad Hussain, and the politician Mahmud Ali, all of whom supported the non-vernacular intelligentsia and could therefore be considered to represent a counter vernacular elite.

The vernacular and counter non-vernacular intelligentsia, tended to see culture and language in secular terms, but not so the non-vernacular and counter vernacular intelligentsia, who prepared a religious perception of culture. Similarly, while members of the vernacular and counter non-vernacular intelligentsia tended to be antagonistic, sometimes aesthetic, and generally tolerant, the non-vernacular and counter-vernacular intelligentsia were usually religious, dogmatic, and at times, communal.

Murshid points out that, when all of East Bengal was agitated by the provisions of a strong center in the Report of the Basic Principles Committee in 1950-1, the main, though weak, resistance in the Assembly came from the opposition consisting mainly of Hindus and a handful of Muslims. Thus at the moment of partition, the politics and economy of Pakistan, including East Bengal, was dominated by non-Bengalis, particularly from the Punjab.

Such non-Bengali domination of the decision-making apparatus provided the political background for the tension between the religious and the secular forces among the intelligentsia. As has already been said in 1954, the movements of protest in East Pakistan received a jolt by the dismissal of the Fazlul Haque government. Henceforth there was a definite rift among the leaders of the United Front—position of Bhasani and Huq vis-à-vis Suhrawardy.

When the United Front was formed during the elections (1954), it was understood that of the three leaders, Bhasani would remain with the party organisation, Huq would be in East Pakistan and Suhrawardy would go to the capital. Suhrawardy consistently wanted to make the Awami League a national party, and himself its leader. His first attempt to do so had been made in 1952 by joining the East Pakistan Awami League with several West Pakistani parties.

Ataur Rehman Khan was the leader of the Awami League Parliamentary Party in East Pakistan. He formed a new Ministry on 6 September 1956, which meant, at least temporarily, the restoration of parliamentary democracy in East Pakistan. Jayanta Kumar Ray points out that, this change of Ministry in East Pakistan upset the delicate balance of power in the National Assembly where the Muslim League-United Front coalition was giving way to a split in the Muslim League that saw the emergence of the Republican Party as very powerful.[6] Prime Minister Chowdhury Mohammed Ali resigned on 8 September, 1956. A Republican-Awami League coalition, with Suhrawardy as the Prime Minister of Pakistan, took office on 12 September, 1956. However, Suhrawardy's efforts to build himself up as a Pakistani national leader required the delicate balancing of conflicting forces.

As Prime Minister of Pakistan from 12 September 1956 to 11 October 1957, he became an ardent supporter of imperialist powers. He went to the extent of openly supporting the Anglo-French-Israeli intervention against Egypt at Suez. Through this shift or deviation from his earlier position, he lost the support of the regional autonomists and the leftists, while his support of Bengali business interests alienated the West Pakistani entrepreneurs. These irreconcilable forces led to a new split in the Awami League and to the fall of Suhrawardy's ministry within thirteen months of its accession to power. After Suhrawardy became the Prime Minister, he had declared that 98 per cent autonomy had been granted to East Pakistan by the 1956 constitution. Suhrawardy also defined the SEATO (South East Asian Treaty Organisation) and CENTO (Central Treaty Organisation) security alliances, but the Awami League had campaigned against the signing of these pacts. For these reasons, the Suhrawardy ministry came under fire from Pakistani businessmen, who alleged that the government was using import licensing as a means of political patronage. The Awami League picked up some right-wing business and industrial support in West Pakistan to fill the vacuum that had been created by the departure of regional autonomists. Similarly, the East Pakistani leftists, for effective participation at the center were dashed when, within a few months of long-awaited national election, martial law was declared, the established political institutions were swept aside, and the civil-military bureaucracy, in which Bengali representation was minimum, assumed power in the country.

In February 1957, at the conference of the Awami League at Kagmari, the conflict between the leadership and the populist cadres were brought to a head on the issue of Prime Minister Suhrawardy's foreign policy. This had led to the ouster of populist "rank-and-file" in the Awami League and of their leader, Maulana Bhasani, who later formed the National Awami Party (NAP). Bhasani visited West Pakistan in early 1957, where he conferred the left-wing leaders and decided to convene an all-Pakistan conference of progressive organizations. This was held in Dhaka on 25 and 26 July 1957, and resulted in the creation of the NAP. The NAP consisted primarily of Awami League dissidents led by Bhasani, whose populist rhetoric and anti-American propaganda now menaced the bureaucratic and military axis at the center. In the retention of the party's hold over the masses, the role of Sheikh Mujib was crucial. Hamza Alavi comments, "...notwithstanding his firm commitments to the elitist group, his rhetoric and even his personal style of life was populist in character."

The India-Pakistan war of 1965 was a pointer to the growing discontent in East Pakistan. The Kashmir problem and the war revealed clearly the distinct attitudes of the East and West Pakistanis and increased their disparities. The difference in the attitude of East Bengali Muslims and West Pakistanis towards India was brought to sharper focus by this Kashmir dispute.

Pakistan from the very beginning viewed the Indian occupation of what it felt, was Muslim Kashmir as a proof of Indian determination to negate the ideological basis of Pakistan. So, when the Indo-Pakistan war occurred in September 1965, the Indian government appeared to have clearly appraised the different outlook of West and East Pakistan in relation to India. During the seventeen day war India discreetly refrained from threatening East Bengal. According to Mizanur Rehman Shelly, the Indian decision to regard East Bengal as a separate entity even in the 1965 war, was based on an informed assessment of the growing strength of the emergent secular, territorial Bengali nationalism in Pakistan's east wing. India welcomed the development that this nationalism held its own, and that the fanatic, religion-based anti-Indian chauvinism of West Pakistan lost much of its effectiveness in East Pakistan. Shelly thinks that the war of 1965 brought into sharp focus the military helplessness and isolation of East Bengal in the event of a total Indo-Pakistan war.

General G.W. Chowdhury has suggested that there was prior "understanding or conspiracy" between some leaders of the Awami League and the government to bring about the secession of East Bengal. After Ayub Khan came to power in 1958 there was complete authoritarian rule in the country until 1962. The political order, as set up by Ayub in his 1962 constitution, gave hardly any scope to the Bengalis for effective and equal participation in national affairs and there was little chance for the Bengalis to develop common national feelings with the West Pakistanis, apart from the religious bond of Islam they had hardly anything common. As in many other parts of Asia and Africa, they became more conscious of region rather than religion. The Islamic ideology, on which Jinnah had based Pakistan, began to fade away, and regional feelings grew fast in East Bengal.

In the opinion of General G.W. Chowdhury, 'Regionalism was the raison d'etre' for the emergence of Bangladesh and East Bengal became a hotbed for political agitation and unrest. Hardly a year passed without Bengalis revolting against alleged maltreatment by the central government.

General G.W. Chowdhury admits that by the 1960s, most of the urban, professional Bengali groups were beginning to consider seriously whether they could or would live together with the western part of the country. He agrees that the greatest blow to Pakistan nationalism came as a result of the Indo-Pakistan war in September 1965. According to an eminent Indian journalist, the Prime Minister Lal Bahadur Shastri decided not to invade East Bengal in 1965 on the advice of the Indian Chief of Army Staff, General J. Chowdhury, who was himself a Bengali.[7] Neither India nor Pakistan could claim victory or be considered defeated in this seventeen day war. In fact, Pakistan with a much smaller army, air and naval force, did quite well in 1965 in comparison with December 1971.

But the war of 1965 disastrously weakened the national bond between East and West Pakistan. According to G.W. Chowdhury, a deep-rooted myth had developed had gripped the people of East Pakistan at the beginning of the war, that if India attacked East Pakistan, West Pakistani soldiers would move up to Delhi. The 1965 war shattered this idea for good. Within one hour of the war, East Pakistan was cut off not only from West Pakistan but from the rest of the world as well, and so the old argument that the defence of East Pakistan lay with the central government no longer held water. Although the war ended in a draw, it had a disastrous effect on Ayub's authority and his image with the armed forces. The six-point programme for maximum regional autonomy for East Bengal was presented in public by the Awami League leader, Sheikh Mujibur Rehman, at the critical psychological juncture marked by the close of the 1965 war. The timing proved highly effective and Bengali nationalism gained strength. G.W. Chowdhury analyses that Mujib's scheme demonstrated Ayub's failure, in spite of a much-publicized campaign, to achieve national integration.

The war of 1965 deeply affected the attitudes of the Bengali intelligentsia. It may be worth connecting the 1965 war with earlier and later transformation in the thoughts of the Bengali intellectuals, particularly the economists of East Pakistan. The newspapers, journals and pamphlets of this period, now available in the libraries of Dhaka, would reveal how far the war of 1965 gave a fillip to the lack of confidence about East Pakistan and the latter's inability to give economic help. It is in this sphere that the phenomenon of internal colonialism needs to be investigated.

Then there was an attempt to kidnap and assassinate General Ayub in December 1967 when he was on tour in East Pakistan. General G.W. Chowdhury comments that although the plot was "unsuccessful and unpublicized", Ayub's image with armed forces immediately became vulnerable. Soon after this, the Pakistan political scene was rocked by the startling news of a case of conspiracy through armed uprisings, and on 2 January, 1968, the government of Pakistan announced the discovery of a plot to bring about the secession of East Pakistan, with Indian help. In collaboration with the First Secretary of the Indian mission in Dhaka, P.N. Ojha, 28 persons were alleged to have been engaged in anti-state activities and were reported to have contacted the Indian officials to get arms and other material aid across the border at Agartala. A few days later, the government announced that Mujib who had been in jail since the movement for Six Points in 1966, was also involved in the Agartala case.

The Six Points were: 1. a federal system of government, parliamentary in nature and based on adult franchise; 2. the federal government to deal only with defence and foreign affairs, all other subjects to be dealt with by the federating state; 3. either two separate but freely convertible currencies for the two parts of the country or one currency for the whole country, in which case effective constitutional measures should be taken to prevent the flight of capital from East to West Pakistan; 4. the power of taxation and revenue collection to be vested in the federating units; 5. separate accounts for foreign exchange earnings of the two parts of the country, under control of the respective governments; 6. the setting—up of a militia or para-military force for East Pakistan. Mujibur's booklet had the sub-title, '6-Point Programme'.[8]

Ayub's provincial governor in East Pakistan, Monem Khan, thought that the most effective way to meet Mujib's challenges was to implicate him in an Indian-inspired conspiracy, which, he expected, would ruin his political career. A British lawyer, T.

Williams, Q.C., who was allowed to come to defend Mujibur Rehman, was assisted by the former Chief Justice of Pakistan, S.M. Murshed, who had been arbitrarily removed by the government. Justice Murshed's indirect support in extending co-operation to Mujib's British lawyer had a further impact on the Bengali public, particularly the intelligentsia and journalists over whom Murshed had tremendous influence, since, his removal as the Chief Justice of East Pakistan had already antagonized public opinion. Therefore, the reaction in Mujib's arrest was most unfavourable and Mujib was a hero overnight. When the drama unfolded to the fullest glare of publicity, the Dhaka newspapers gave banner headlines to the proceedings of the case. Compared to the pre-independence days in undivided India, the Agartala case had given the same impetus to the cause of Bengali nationalism in Pakistan, in the same way as Jinnah's vigorous publicity campaign against Congress rule in the Muslim minority provinces in 1937-9 gave to the cause of Pakistan. Rounaq Jahan agrees with G.W. Chowdhury that throughout 1966-8, while Sheikh Mujib was in prison, his popularity increased, and the Agartala conspiracy case instead of destroying his support, helped to build it by magnifying his role as the champion of Bengali rights. By early 1969 when Mujib was freed from prison and was welcomed in Dhaka by an unprecedented show of popular support, he stood well above the other leaders and even above his own party. The election of 1970, in which his party won 167 out of 169 East Pakistani seats, institutionalized his standing as the supreme leader in East Pakistan.

A close look at East Pakistan of 1950s and 1960s would show that while the political thoughts of Suhrawardy, Fazlul Haque, Bhasani or Sheikh Mujib were influential, they had strong social, economic and intellectual roots; it would be a mistake to identify the language movement alone with the origins of the entire freedom struggle in Bangladesh, as is sometimes done in popular literature.

Prior to the partition of 1947, one may note the attitude of the CPI about the partition of India, because, the Awami League, born in Pakistan born in 1949, had formed a link with the party. Maulana Abdul Hamid Khan Bhasani called a convention of Muslim League workers at Narayangung on 23 June 1949. The convention laid the foundation for the most powerful opposition political party to challenge the authority of the Muslim League. On that day many of the leaders opposed to the Muslim League were in jail.

The convention formed a new party which was named the East Pakistan Awami Muslim League. Maulana Bhasani became its founder-President. Ataur Rahman Khan, Abdus Salam Khan and Abdul Mansoor Ahmed were elected Vice-Presidents. Shamsul Huq was elected General Secretary, Sheikh Mujibur Rahman, Rafiqul Ahsan and Khondakar Mustaque Ahmed were elected Joint Secretaries.[9]

The present sovereign and independent state of Bangladesh was earlier known as East Bengal. In East Bengal, a few weekly journals were published, and it cannot be ascertained whether all the weekly magazines had political ideals—but '*Dhaka Prakash*' was an ancient journal published from Dhaka and the main work of this magazine was to focus on the role of the All India Congress in contemporary politics.[10]

Abul Hashim narrates that, one evening, as early as January 1944, Maulana Akram Khan and his son Khayrul Anam took him to the district office of the Indian Communist party in a car.[11] There he saw for the first time P.C. Joshi, the General Secretary of C.P.I.[12] Maulana was very happy to talk to the Communist party leader. The Communist Party had demanded a federal state of India, where each of the fifteen different linguistic communities would have the right of self-determination, including the right to secede. On the basis of this independent demand, the main slogan of the Communist Party was that, the 'League, Congress, party' should combine against British imperialism. But due to the policy of communal differences emphasized by the British government and the failure of the leadership of the Muslim League and the Congress, communal conflict reached its heights allover India and when India's partition became inevitable, the Communist party was also forced to accept the reality. The party in East Bengal, too, under the instruction of the all-India party took a stand in favour of the demand for Pakistan.

The leaders of Bengal Communist Party gave the guarantee of co-operation in organizing the Muslim League as a democratic and progressive political party. This was how Abul Hashim and others started communication with the Communist Party.[13] The pioneer work, *Nationalism and Democracy in East Pakistan* (1968) by Professor Jayanta Kumar Ray studies the political situation in East Pakistan immediately after the partition. Studying the Pakistani situation in 1968-70, Professor Jayanta Kumar Ray, a social scientist from Kolkata, wrote his book,[14] and the book is a bright illustration of research work through area-study. At the outset, he suggests that the problem of East Pakistan was two-fold. In the first place, since the emergence of Pakistan as an independent state, those who dominated the Central Government, remaining predominantly East Pakistani in composition, had consistently tried to impose a cultural, economic and political hegemony upon East Pakistan. The relative strength of cultural, economic and political motivations in this hegemonial design might be a matter of debate.

Secondly, minorities in East Pakistan—Buddhists, Christians and, by far the most numerous, Hindus—had been systematically discriminated against and pushed into the neighbouring areas of India. The degree and extent of discrimination varied by time and place but it had occurred continuously.[15]

As political consciousness increased rapidly in East Pakistan, the ruling circle started a conspiracy, the first victim of which was Liaquat Ali Khan. In the month of March, 1951, Major General Akbar Khan of the Centre decided to remove the normal government in Bangladesh and Prime Minister Liaquat Ali Khan, who was not their favourate. East Bengal admitted six non-Bengalis within its quota of members of the Constituent Assembly of Pakistan; so that Liaquat Ali Khan came to occupy an East Bengal seat in the Constituent Assembly. From Jayanta Ray's account one can get an idea of the fact that even within the Assembly Liaquat had his open critics such as Dhirendra Lal Dhar. The Assembly was taking inordinate delay in making a proper constitution for Pakistan, and gradually a feeling grew that conspiracies were the only way to remove the undesirable people and gain political power. The result was the martyrdom of Prime Minister Liaquat Ali Khan on 16th October, 1951, when he was giving a speech in open daylight in the main office of the army cantonment in Rawalpindi. The ruling circle did not have the honesty and courage to publish the Investigation Report of Liaquat murder.

After Liaquat's murder, the Punjabi bureaucrat Gulam Mohammad and government servant Chowdhury Mohammed Ali became the Governor General and the Finance Minister of Pakistan respectively.

The Liaquat murder conspiracy was so-well conceived that the assassin had to die on the spot according to plan. Otherwise, the real identity of the conspirators might be revealed through the confessions of the assassin and this was the result of a hateful, consolidated conspiracy of the military and civil rulers.

Liaquat's wife declared unequivocally for several years at public meetings that she suspected the bureaucracy of hatching up a conspiracy to assassinate Liaquat. She was insistent on this point till she succumbed to the machinations of the bureaucracy that neutralized her opposition with the offer of a job of an Ambassador to her. According to Professor Jayanta Kumar Ray, Liaquat's exit saw succession in Pakistan being settled by an uneasy compromise that had in it all the seeds of disintegration.[16]

After witnessing the palace conspiracy and the international network involved with it, the progressive-minded people and the leftists in East Pakistan became active. The Youth League, the *Ganatantric Dal* and the progressives within the Awami Muslim League became irritated and vocal against this palace conspiracy. The ideological conspiracy within the party in the decades of the sixties that originated in the Great Debate' between the Chinese and the Soviet camp, also had a direct effect on the leftists of the country.

Kamruddin Ahmed, a resident of Dhaka, a well-known legal luminary of that period, trails back the socio-economic and socio-political history of East Pakistan to ancient times and gives it a new angle by identifying certain trends in the direction of social change in East Pakistan. His book, *A Socio-Political History of Bengal and the Birth of Bangladesh* (1967) gives a general overview of the situation in East Pakistan from ancient times to the birth of Bangladesh. Kamruddin Ahmed in his book, *A Socio-Political History of Bengal* (1967), argues that, due to different climate and other conditions, the life of the people of East Bengal was completely distinct from that of the western region in all its social aspects. Economically also, the eastern region was different from the western wing, and while in 1947, East Bengal was a developing agricultural country in the process of industrialization, West Pakistan had only a pastoral economy. The agricultural products of the east wing were mainly tea, jute, rice and it was for years the only exporter of jute in the world.

Lastly, Tariq Ali, a Pakistani who made several visits to East Pakistan, was a sympathizer of leftist movements in Pakistan, and dealt with economic elements of inherent contradictions within the Pakistan state, which made Pakistan difficult to survive during the first twenty-five years of its formation. Tariq Ali in his two books, *Pakistan: Military Rule or People's Power*? (1970) and *Can Pakistan Survive? The Death of a State* (1972), have probed into the basic dissensions inherent within the society and state of Pakistan. Tariq Ali agrees with Kamruddin Ahmed that East Pakistan or East Bengal was completely unlike the western part of the country, and the only common link between east and west was religion. But the religious bond faded into insignificance vis-à-vis a succession of momentous political and economic events. Other factors which supposedly united the two parts of the country were the English language and the Pakistan International Airlines, which had nothing to do with the toiling masses in both East and West Pakistan. According to Ali, in East Bengal the establishment of Pakistan had simply resulted in non-Bengalis, mainly from West Pakistan, filling the place of departed Hindus. The industrialists used the foreign exchange from jute earnings of East Pakistan to industrialise West Pakistan, and this explosion was bound to provoke a nationalist response. He further characterizes the Awami League as the party of the urban petty bourgeoisie, and its propaganda on the national question had won it considerable support in the major cities of East Pakistan. While the strength of the peasant organizations was minimal in West Pakistan, in the east they were fairly strong, having an active tradition of militancy.

These three authors, although writing in different dimensions, have some observations common amongst them. Since all of them have written from the period much before the birth of Bangladesh, and did not view independence of East Pakistan as an accomplished fact, they did not see the East Pakistani situation as anything more than a problem that might give rise to secessionist tendency. The authors focus on the physical distance between East and West Pakistan, the discrimination made by the Pakistan government towards the East Pakistanis, the economic exploitation of the east by the west, specially with regard to the policy towards the jute industries, the oppression of the minority communities in East Pakistan, and many such other instances. The authors are worried about the recurrence of military dictatorships and without probing into the causality of this event, they try to narrate the problems and dangers of the failure of democracy in East Pakistan, where it was found that each time the results of the democratic elections were suppressed and military rule followed. It is apparent that the elite was not visualizing the prospect of creating a separate nation-state until the end of 1960s. It was the war between Pakistan and India in 1965, which formed the watershed in this matter, and gave East Pakistan a separate identity for the first time.

In a book published immediately after the independence of Bangladesh, and named, *Can Pakistan Survive? The Death of a State* (1972), Ali devotes one full chapter on the Baluch uprising in East Pakistan in 1972-3. He narrates how people in the province of Baluchistan, which was quite unlike the other parts of Pakistan, became determined to separate itself after Pakistan's independence, and the Bhutto government could suppress the guerilla warfare of the Baluchs, who lacked the foreign support that East Pakistan thrived on. Although Tariq Ali was a full sympathizer of the Baluch cause, the failure of the Baluch uprisings indicate two facts about the reasons for the success of East Pakistan: in the first place, the role of the elite inside and outside the country which led to the formation of a strong public opinion in favour of East Pakistan and secondly, the positive factor of foreign intervention and help in the secession of East Pakistan. These factors have been highlighted by both Tariq Ali and Ahmed.

II

A good body of literature has evolved around the 1952 language movement, which proves its multidimensional character. Badruddin Umar's three volumes on, *Purba Banglar Bhasha Andolon o Tatkalin Rajniti* (1995) has a detailed view of the language movement of 1952, from a pro-Bengali bias, and offers a valuable insight on the birth of the language movement and analyses its nature and class character. *Bhasha Andolon Dalilpatra* by Ratanlal Chkrobarty supplies some primary evidence regarding the victims of the 1952 movement and there are numerous other writings, elaborating on the sacrifice of the martyrs.

Rounaq Jahan in her work, *Pakistan: Failure in National Integration* (1972), places the Pakistan problem in a broader South Asian context and locates the situation in Pakistan in a post-colonial setup. Again, Tazeen M. Murshid in her book, *The Sacred and the Secular Muslim Discourses 1871-1977* (1995), elaborates Rounaq Jahan's model when she points out that the vernacular intelligentsia failed to compel their opponents to arrive at a political understanding despite the numerical strength of their supporters, because of their inability to control the army.

Rounaq Jahan points out that, the two-economy thesis was first propounded in 1956 at a special conference of the economists meeting in Dhaka to discuss the First Five Year Plan, and it forms the intellectual platform on which the economic necessities of the autonomy movement was forwarded. An analysis of the economic objectives of the second five-year plan, pointed out that, a better, richer and happier life for every man and woman in Pakistan, was the chief objective of the Second Five Year Plan.

When Ayub Khan took over the reins of the government in 1958, the new regime started taking keen interest in the economic planning. A series of steps were taken including the re-organisation of the planning body of the country, to set the house in order.[17] According to Mohammad Tariq Wasim, during this period of a decade or so, Pakistan achieved a sustained rate of growth of 5 per cent, the total increase in income was 160, exports rose by 8 per cent per annum, and increase in agricultural sector was 4.5 per cent per annum.[18]

With political stability in the country and over-keenness and willingness to heed and act according to the advice of the foreign governments, there was a large influx of foreign aid. The development in Pakistan was a direct function of foreign aid. Foreign assistance formed 35 per cent, 50 per cent and 26 per cent of total investments in the 1st, 2nd and 3rd Plans.

2/3 of private industrial investment was controlled by individuals and families drawn from a few trading communities. According to Mohammed Tariq Waseem, this concentration of economic power was translatable into political influence. This meant that those who had arrived wanted to retain high protection against imports, prevent any new investments in their industry, and thus maintained and retained their monopoly position and high profits.

Mason offers the other side of the prosperity in industrialization. He says that industrialization had been accompanied by large inefficiencies and very considerable misdirection of investments.[19] Moreover, the malpractices by them cost the nation millions of rupees in terms of taxes, etc. According to Papanek, "Pakistan industrialists hide their profits by various devices—Survey data in this area (profits) are unreliable, incomplete and grossly understated". There could hardly be any competition in Pakistan because of current aggregate excess demand vis-à-vis limited amount of supply.

According to Mumtaz Hasan, in spite of considerable progress registered in many fields of the economic and social life in the First Plan and earlier, the economy was still far from a position of strength. Primary material, such as newspaper clippings for research reveals that, the average income per person was about ₹ 243/- per annum in Pakistan as against ₹ 10,000/- in America and the average expectation of life in Pakistan was 32 years compared with 65 in the USA and around 70 in the Scandinavian countries. Finally, it has been pointed out, there was overcrowding in cities as well as rural areas.

The Second Plan aimed at accelerating the momentum already gained ("TAKE-OFF" STAGE), and ensuring the steady advance of the economy to the stage where it could itself generate the resources necessary for its continued growth. A study of the Five Year Plans of Pakistan would point out the economic and political situation in the country.

The basic objective of the plan was to bring about maximum feasible increase in the rate of production in the country. New canals, roads, factories and power houses would be built to stimulate economic activity.[20] New land would be brought under cultivation.[21] Substantial increase would take place in the acreage of improved land. Health facilities would be expanded.[22] Educational opportunities would be expanded and improved substantially.[23]

In analyzing national income, it was said that the aim that they had set before them was dubbing of the average income per head within a generation, and reaching a stage of development wherein further growth became automatic.[24] Mumtaz Hasan further elaborates that, as a result of the Second Plan the national income of Pakistan was expected to increase by 20 per cent. But gradually, as the country's resources expand and more money is invested in improving the agriculture, in putting up new factories and in buildings, dams, the income would also rise correspondingly.

So far as East Wing Development is concerned, the plan would make a concerted effort to accelerate the rate of development in East Pakistan and the less developed regions of West Pakistan. East Pakistan, in spite of notable strides made since independence, was still relatively more underdeveloped than West Pakistan. Economic and social over-heads such as transport, communications, power and water supplies which constituted the framework of future economic growth were comparatively lacking there. The Second Plan would provide for the creation of these overheads and made accelerated growth in this province possible.[25]

The programme to be carried out in East Pakistan by the Central and East Pakistan governments were estimated at about more than two and half times the actual expenditure incurred in East Pakistan in the public sector during the period of the First Plan.[26] The special and Frontier regions of West Pakistan—which were characterized by extreme poverty—had also been looked after by the Plan.[27] These were to be developed at as rapid a rate as possible.[28] The development expenditure in these regions would be around ₹ 50 crore during the entire plan period.[29]

A better, richer and happier life for every man and woman in Pakistan was the chief objective of the Second Five Year Plan.[30] The plan was a blue-print for the most effective utilization of the country's resources in order to promote the welfare of the people as a whole.[31] Mumtaz Hasan points out that, in spite of considerable progress registered in many fields of their economic and social life in the First Plan period and earlier, the economy was still far from a position of strength.[32] The living standards in the country were amongst the lowest in the world.[33] The average income per person was about ₹ 243/- per annum in Pakistan as against ₹ 10,000/- in America.[34] Amongst the Asian countries, Egypt, Iran, Iraq, India, Japan, Ceylon and Lebanon were ahead of Pakistan, some of them far ahead.[35]

The Pakistanis were woefully deficient in hospitals, doctors and nurses.[36] Only about 10 per cent of the population could read and write.[37] The pressure on the land resources of Pakistan was increasing on account of the rapid growth of population in the country.[38] Finally, there was overcrowding in cities and rural areas as well.[39]

Successive Presidents and their outlook on Bangladesh: President Field Marshall Mohammed Ayub Khan announced that the proposal for a joint defence pact between India and Pakistan did not violate the non-alignment policy professed by India. According to 'Morning News', with the goodwill and understanding between the two countries, an arrangement could be made by which people living in the area could defend the sub-continent, he said,[40] while at a press meet at the Dhaka Airport on his arrival from Rawalpindi, on the afternoon on January 21, to undertake an extensive tour of East Pakistan.[41] According to this report, the crux of the whole thing was that Indian and Pakistani forces, facing each other at the moment, could be released to defend their respective territories, once differences between the two nations were resolved.[42]

Pakistan's stand, he said, had been that these differences were solved by India and Pakistan and some sort of an arrangement could be made by which the two countries could jointly defend the sub-continent.[43] Another report of the same newspaper noted that, foreign exchange bonus had been reduced on the export of yarn from 20 to 10 per cent, according to a decision by the Governors' conference at Dhaka.[44]

The conference, second in Dhaka, was held at the Government House. The Governors' Conference that was presided over by Field Marshall Mohammed Ayub Khan began at 6-15 pm in the Conference Room of the Government House in Dhaka on January 21, 1960.[45] He was flanked by his cabinet Ministers at a horse shoe conference table.

The two Governors, Zakir Hussain and Akhtar Hussain sat at a separate table facing the President. All these events were a prelude to the war of 1965. In 1965, after the India-Pakistan war, a law named, 'Enemy Properties Act', was made in contemporary East Pakistan. According to that law the Bangladeshi Hindus who left for India, even for a short period, were marked as enemies by the government, which seized their land and properties in its own hand and distributed among its own people as it liked. Taking advantage of this act, in many places Muslims displaced the Hindus from their own soil and captured their land as enemy property. Those who had thought that the Awami League was in reality an anti-communal and democratic political party expected that, after the establishment of the state of Bangladesh, the Enemy Properties Act would be annulled and the Hindus, whose properties had been captured through this law, would be given back their proprietary rights. The Awami League government, however, changed the name of the 'Enemy Properties Act' into 'Vested Properties Act'. This new act was nothing but new wine in old bottles. This came as a profound disappointment to the Hindus of East Pakistan. Historian Ratanlal Chakrobarty in his works has dealt extensively in this matter.

In the Pakistan period and afterwards, the ruling circle were trying to misuse religion and the Islamic sentiments in order to preserve their authority. In 1968, Ayub Khan argued in a speech that all regional languages had to be integrated to innovate a great Pakistani language.[46] To illustrate this point, in 1968, the Academic Council of Dhaka University recommended that the Bengali language should be reformed. But in the same period (1947-71), a strong secular sentiment was taking grip of the Bengalee mind, and the civic society was moving against all fundamentalist dogmas. As a part of this resistance campaign, in July 1968, the writers' union organized a five-day function in honour of poet Nazrul. Abul Hashim delivered an important speech on this occasion, and observed that those who advocated a boycott of Rabindranath's songs on the pretext of following Islam and the ideology of Pakistan, were not only foolish but also mischievous, who understood neither Islam nor Rabindranath, and wanted to serve a special interest by denouncing Rabindranath Tagore.[47]

However, during the lengthy month of struggle for freedom, the Pakistani army had settled themselves in Bangladesh, and their continuous presence gave a strong fillip to fundamentalist politics in Bangladesh. The soldiers performed the worst kind of genocide on the Bengalis, both the Hindus and the Muslims, the main target of attack being the religious minorities and Hindus. They even considered the Muslim of Bangladesh as 'kafer's. During that crisis in 1971, the members of the religious and political parties like Jamaat-e-Islami, Muslim League, Nezam-e-Islami and others, in the name of preserving Islam and maintaining the integrity of Pakistan, preserved the Pakistani army to perform genocide, violence on women and *dacoities* and they themselves actively participated in the process.

Reference may be made in this context to the writings of prominent sculptor Ferdousi Priyobhashini, who was a prisoner in the freedom fight of Bangladesh at Khulna. She was a prisoner in the hands of the Pakistani army and its agents for nine months in the Crescent Jute Mill. She was a eye-witness to the brutal killings, mass genocide and destroyal by the army. She saw how the bodies of the Bengalis were dissected to two pieces by a blade used for cutting jute. This operation inside the jute mills have been compared to the process of guillotine in the French Revolution of 1789.[48]

Bangladesh became independent in December 1971, after a nine-month war that pitted Bengali-dominated East Pakistan against West Pakistan. The West's army, with its appeal to Islamic unity, had the support of many of East Pakistan's fundamentalist parties. The most extreme of these was the Jamaat-e-Islami, whose student wing became the main source of a pro-army paramilitary body called Al Badr, which was led by Motiur Rehman Nzami, leader of the third largest party of present Bangladesh, Jamaat-e-Islami. Its members are alleged, among other atrocities, to have abducted and murdered dozens of senior journalists and academics. Shariar Kabir, the head of the present '*Ghatak Dalal Nirmul* Committee', says that he has "no doubt" that the case against Nizami and his associates would stand up in a court of law, and wants government to set up a tribunal.

The committee opened liaison offices in various parts of Dhaka city after April, in the offices of '*Jamaat-e-Islami'*. In association with this move at the center, local branches and student organizations under their influence formed action groups to counter guerilla attacks and execute the supporters of the liberation struggle. The main groups were:

(i) *Razakars*: Abbas Ali Khan started organizing this group in Bogra.
(ii) *Al Badar*: (*Islami Chhatra Sangha*), the student wing of *Jamaat-e-Islami* formed the nucleus of this group and Madrasa students were the members and
(iii) *Al Shams* (the student wing of Muslim League, responsible for massacre of the students in Chittagong).

The three groups having organized the executive wing of the Peace Committee, co-operated with the Pakistani army, and led terrorist actions against the supporters of the liberation, both in urban and rural areas No less than 5000 execution wards were their creations, to butcher the sympathizers of the liberation struggle.

Finally on 16 December 1971 when victory was earned, the occupiers of Bangladesh and the fundamentalist Muslims took shelter in Pakistan or went into hiding inside the state, waiting for their chance of revival. Golam Azam was deprived of the citizenship of Bangladesh since he made alliance with the enemies of independence. He lived in Pakistan with a Pakistani passport and waited for his chance to start fundamentalist misdeeds in independent Bangladesh.

In November 1971, Golam Azam, the former *Ameer* of *Jamaat-e-Islami*, went from Lahore to East Pakistan to join a meeting of the central committee of Jamaat-e-Islami. He appealed to all Pakistanis to forget their political affiliations and to unite against the Bangladesh freedom movement. After Bangladesh gained freedom on 16 December 1971, Golam Azam was deprived of citizenship in Bangladesh, and came over to settle in Pakistan; waiting for a chance to revive fundamentalism in Bangladesh.

General G.W. Chowdhury in his book, *The Last Days of United Pakistan* (1974), offers a different viewpoint when he admits that he was a believer in "one Pakistan" and that the most serious challenge to Pakistan's nationalism was founded only on economic disparity between its two wings. Similar view may be found in the book, *The Betrayal of East Pakistan* (1998), written by another Pakistani General A.A.K. Niazi, who further tries to prove that, "the disintegration of Pakistan was an arranged capitulation.".

Ayesha Jalal in her work, *The State of Martial Rule*: *The Origins of Pakistan's Political Economy of Defence* (1990), published earlier than her most acclaimed book, *The Sole Spokesman Jinnah, the Muslim League and the Demand for Pakistan* (1994) analyses the insecurity of the new-born state of Pakistan, and its lack of industrial and economic resources, to explain the reasons for exploitative tendencies by one part of the state on another. Jalal attempts to show why the military and the bureaucracy came to assume the dominant role in the decision-making within the state-structure, through a close and careful scrutiny of the different ways in which the interplay of the regional and international factors influenced domestic politics and economy, distorting the relations between the center and the provinces in particular.

There is yet another discourse that deals with the growth of political parties in East Pakistan and identifies the growth of national politics. There are some writers who try to assess the role of the foreign countries in the liberation war of Bangladesh. Mizanur Rehman Shelly in his book, *Emergence of a new nation in a multi-polar world: Bangladesh* (1979), thought that the war of 1965 brought into sharp focus the military helplessness and isolation of East Bengal in the event of a total Indo-Pakistan war. According to this group of historians and litterateurs, the 1965 war acted as a catalyst in awakening the anger of the East Pakistanis against General Ayub Khan's oppression, and this feeling gained strength to reach a climax in 1971. An important luminary of this period was Professor Azizur Rehman Mallik, who in his book, *Amar Jibankatha o Bangladesher Muktishangram* (1995) brought into focus the importance of world public opinion on the question of East Pakistan and described how he delivered lectures at different universities in New York, Columbia, Chicago, Harvard and many other places within a period of thirty-six days (in the year 1971), with the task of creating a general consciousness amongst the Americans on the Bangladesh-issue, of acquiring the support of different ambassadors by meeting them and simultaneously helped ordinary people in the United States by lecturing in different meetings. Professor Anisuzzaman in one of his works, *Amar Ekattor* (1998) narrates how in his days of exile, he along with others traveled in different cities of India and delivered speeches to create public opinion in favour of freedom movement of Bangladesh.

III

There are innumerable other writings that reveal the varying attitudes of the writers and intellectuals towards the East Pakistan movement, a few of which have been named here, but a close analysis and classification of their thought is also required. As Christopher Hill comments in his book, *The Intellectual Origins of the English Revolution*, "Ideals were all-important for the individuals whom they impelled into action;". A study of the role of the intelligentsia as a key-factor in the emergence of Bangladesh, which propagated the economic, social and political harassment of the 'Bengalis', by the West Pakistanis to the outside world, going back to the 1940s, 1950s and 1960s may be significant for an appraisal of the factor of emergence of Bangladesh as a new nation in Asia.

The language movement is an incomparable source in the rise and growth of Bengali nationalism. Language and culture is most important in the self-development of a nation's soul. It will not be too much to say that the language movement played a significant role in the world history, so far as its own language, culture and the growth of civilization is concerned.

Pakistan was a fascinating laboratory for studying the construction of a state.[49] Ayesha Jalal argues that, alternatively between detailed and more general levels of analysis, there was the interplay of domestic, regional and international factors and how it weakened the position of parties and politicians within the evolving structure of the Pakistani state by tilting the institutional balance in favour of the bureaucracy and the military. The focus on institutional imbalances places the question of 'ethnicity' and provincialism in an altogether different light.

Pakistan government, from its very inception, wanted to offer certain privileges to the intelligentsia. The government wanted to drain the ordinary people. If the intelligentsia became a part of the ordinary people, then they would draw the attention of the commoners, and that would be a hindrance to carry out the drain. At the other end, if the intelligentsia spread the message of the greatness of Pakistan, then the drain can be carried out smoothly. Since the intelligentsia was not solvent enough, and they were fond of solvency, so they were attracted easily by small promises. Improvement in jobs, prizes for writing books, chance to visit a foreign country—all these offers made by the Pakistan government separated the ordinary people from the intelligentsia, and they were successful in many respects. The intelligentsia class in the society—writers, educationists, reporters and many important people among them—often prospered after the establishment of the state of Pakistan. They were Bengalis by way of nationalities.

There was much confusion regarding modernity and objectives. The followers of Islam were relatively backward, in comparison a part of the youth were obsessed with the idea of modernity, and the imperialists were behind all such confusion. The Pakistanis stressed that, there was no place for foreign culture and idealism in Pakistan.

Sirajul Islam Chowdhury speaks about only one section of the

Bengali Muslim intelligentsia. Another section of intelligentsia was the majority community and constituted the youth. Sirajul Islam Chowdhury further points out that, in the year 1948 it was evident that Pakistan would fail completely to realize the expectations, almost from the same time when the state was established. Even before the establishment of the state of Pakistan, not that all the intellectuals in the country accepted the communal politics of Bangladesh.

Revolt could not reveal always, and so gradually it became insurmountable. 21st February, 1952, introduced many changes in the outlook of the intelligentsia, especially in case of literature and industry. The viewpoint of the Muslim middle class in Bangladesh was directed towards the west, they had a difficult psychology, and a question was raised whether their mother tongue was Bengali.

The western rulers were much adamant about the Bengali language. It is a possibility that their self-interest may be hampered, but when they could not silence the movement, then Bengali was accepted as the state language in the constitutions of 1956 and 1962. In the 1960s, the Pakistani government constructed a dam in the hills to produce electricity, and the land of thousands of Chakmas was submerged.

Although from the middle of the '50s, the Bengali economists were steadily writing the story of how East Pakistan was being treated as a colony by its western part, it is important to note that, the famous essay on 'two-nation-two-economy' by Rehman Sobhan was published in 'The Concept of Pakistan', on January 6, 1965.

Here is an attempt to analyse some of the works of the writers on the problem of Bengalis, of how they viewed a new nation in the making. Jayanta Ray's book, *Democracy and Nationalism on Trial a Study of East Pakistan* (1968), studies the state of affairs in East Pakistan for the first twenty years and offers an adequate understanding of a complex problem of insurgency in East Pakistan. In this book, Ray seeks to analyse the deep-rooted and widespread frustrations of the new Bengali Muslim elite in East Pakistan.[50]

Ray traces how the eclipse of the Muslim League led towards a military dictatorship.[51] While under the military law administration, the failure of the theory and practice of Basic Democracy gave rise to the movement for an autonomous East Bengal. He suggested that the problem in East Pakistan was two-fold: in the first place, since the emergence of Pakistan as an independent state, those who dominated the central government, remaining consistently West Pakistani in composition, continuously tried to impose a cultural, economic and political hegemony upon East Pakistan. Secondly, the minorities in East Pakistan were systematically discriminated against and pushed into the neighbouring areas of India. Although the extent of discrimination varied, it occurred continuously. Ray asserts that the West Pakistani leaders sometimes unleashed a large-scale campaign for uprooting East Pakistan's minorities with a view to furthering a domination of East Pakistan.

According to Jayanta Kumar Ray, the factors responsible for the distrust of the West Pakistani rulers towards East Pakistan and their attempt to keep East Pakistanis under subservience are many and complex.[52] According to him, the West Pakistani Muslims tended to look down upon the Bengali Muslims because the latter happened to be mostly the descendants of converts from Hinduism, while the former claimed to be descendants of Muslims coming from West Asia.[53]

Ray is of the opinion that, since 1947, East Pakistan had been a scene of restructuring of the elite and of an outburst of cultural-political-economic aspirations of the new elite.[54] The Hindu elite of the pre-1947 era was replaced by the Muslim elite mainly as a result of violence, which either destroyed or pushed out the members of the older elite into the neighbouring state of India. The new Pakistani elite, however, found it almost impossible to achieve its legitimate goal because of the use of force and intrigues by the West Pakistani ruling authorities spearheading the military-bureaucratic complex. This book by Ray also seeks to analyse the emergence and frustrations of the new Bengali Muslim elite in East Pakistan.[55]

Tariq Ali has written two books on the east Pakistani problem: *Pakistan: Military Rule or People's Power?* (1970), *Can Pakistan Survive? The Death of a State* (1972) and an article, 'Pakistan and Bangladesh: Problems and Prospects', in *Explosion in a Subcontinent: India, Pakistan, Bangladesh and Ceylon*, edited by Robin Blackburn. Ali agrees with Kamruddin Ahmed that East Pakistan or East Bengal was completely unlike the western part of the country, and the only common link between East and West was religion. But the religious bond faded into insignificance vis-à-vis a succession of momentous political and economic events. Other factors which supposedly united the two parts of the country were the English language and Pakistan International Airlines, which had nothing to do with the toiling masses in both East and West Pakistan.

The industrialists used the foreign exchange from jute earnings of East Pakistan to industrialise West Pakistan, and this exploitation was bound to provide a nationalist response. While the strength of the peasant organizations was minimal in West Pakistan, in the east they were fairly strong, having an active tradition of militancy. Therefore, studying the Pakistani situation in 1970, Tariq Ali admits that the national question had emerged as an extremely important facet of Pakistan's political life, because of the economic exploitation of East Pakistan by West Pakistani capitalists.

The writings of Professor Asim Roy in highlighting the nature and history of Islam in Bengal, argues that, the most important form of external challenge to Islam emanates from the twin pressures of westernization spreading through globalisation, as also a related process of an effective elimination of Communist threat to western capitalism in the wake of the Soviet debacle.[56] According to Roy, one seminal component of such profound changes is the resurrection of the old Islamic threat in the form of Islamic "fundamentalism".[57]

According to Syed Anwar Hosain, although the concept of Islamic resurgence had its origins long ago, it became more prominent during the 1970s.[58] Actually, 'militant Islam' is a kind of response to 'militant colonialism' and 'militant Christianity', imposed on Muslim countries through western expansionism in the nineteenth centuries. Syed Anwar Hosain explains that, this western intrusion in the context of Bangladesh, elicited three grades of responses: acculturationist, normative and neo-normative. Syed Anwar Hosain maintains that, Sir Syed Ahmad Khan (1817-98) and Syed Amir Ali represented the acculturationist trend in British India. Acculturationist Islam generally accepted the western definition of reality and sought to reform and redefine the Islamic system to fit into the models and norms thus appropriated. Acculturationist Islam again had two forms, nationalist and secular, both of which flourished under colonial rule. Its impact, however, on present-day Bangladesh is only marginal.

The term normativist usually refers to those Muslim traditionalists who never waver in the theory of rejection of the western ideals as alien and ungodly. Typical examples of this were the Wahabi and the Faraizi movement in British India. In present-day Bangladesh, the 'Jamaat-e-Islami', the 'Nezam-e-Islami', the 'Khilafat Andolon' etc. are all champions of what has been described as neo-normative Islam.

The neo-normatives seek to modernize Islam but refuse to revitalize it. They strive to develop an Islamic identity that is considered at once Muslim and equally relevant to the modern world and the neo-normatives are consistent in affirming that Islam is the norm by which all reality should be measured and everyone judged. The most notable advocate of neo-normative Islam was Hasan al-Banna of Egypt who founded the Islamic brotherhood movement, and preached that Islam must impinge on public policy and must be intimately concerned with all aspects of the idealized past and also the vanguard of a future yet to be revealed.

Khomenian Iran, Palestanian Al-Hamas and Hizabullah, the National Islamic Front of Sudan, Islamic Brotherhood of Egypt, Islamic revolutionaries in Algeria, Talibans and other Mujahideen in Afganisthan, Indonesia, India and Malyasia, and religiously concerned and sensitive Muslims in the western countries, like USA, UK and similar groups in other Asian and European countries are objects of fierce curiosity and controversies of journalists and politicians.

It shows that Islamic fundamentalism is at present a world-wide phenomenon, and is going to put its imprint on economy and politics. Fundamentalism in Bangladesh is only a chapter in the universal movement. It is noteworthy that, there is an extraordinary degree of vagueness and confusion about what constitutes Islamic fundamentalism. Asim Roy admits that, "Islamic fundamentalism" does exist, as various Muslim groups take advantage of its flexibility in order to serve their own interests. Hence, the real challenge in studying Islam is to bring out clearly the non-religious precepts intermingled with the religious. Only then fundamentalism can be understood in its proper perspective.

Unfortunately, in most cases, 'fundamentalists' are far away from the basic principles of the religion they claim to espouse. In reality, the leading Islamic fundamentalists are mostly using Islam as a political tool rather than trying to return to the fundamentals of Islam. This has resulted into a widespread unrest among the masses of the Islamic world, who are now totally confused. The cries of suffering, anguish and anger arising from the continuing tragedy of vagueness of destination, the confusion of the goal to be achieved and the path to be followed, remain drowned under the ocean of arguments of the so-called Resurgent Islam. The debates and discussions on the so-called fundamentalist Islam, both at popular and scholarly levels, have conduced to foster and create monolithic, but stereotyped and imaginary, concepts of Islam. As Edward Said says, a reason for widespread unrest in the Muslim world is the betrayal of the Muslim masses by their elites.

The Sunni fundamentalist Muslim society for Saudi Arabia supports monarchy and Shia fundamentalist society in Iran supports republicanism. Again, Gaddafi in Syria analyses himself as an Islamic socialist. All these leaders are not fundamentalists of one type: but certain features are common to them all—such as the absence of the right to give independent opinions, of freedom of speech, the existence of a despotic state-power ruling over everything. These characteristics are to be found in all fundamentalist societies and states—both Islamic and non-Islamic.

The fundamentalists do not believe in democracy, and fundamentalism has emerged as a threat to orderly growth of arts and culture, history and civilization in many parts of the world. In their oft-propagated theocratic state, religious minorities are relegated to the status of second-class citizens. Under constant pressure from the fundamentalists, religious minorities in these countries are already being discriminated in employment, business and in the enjoyment of other fundamental rights.

Notes

1. Jayanta Kumar Ray, *Democracy and Nationalism on Trial A Study of East Pakistan (*Indian Institute of Advanced Study, Simla, 1968) p. 1.
2. *Ibid.*, p. 1.
3. Tariq Ali, *Can Pakistan Survive? The Death of a State.*
4. Hamza Alavi, "The State in Postcolonial Societies", in Kathleen Gough and Hari P. Sharma (edited) *Imperialism and Revolution in South Asia* (Monthly Review Press).
5. *The Sacred and the Secular Muslim Discourses Bengal 1871-1977.*
6. Jayanta Kumar Ray, *Democracy and nationalism on Trial A Study of East Pakistan*, p. 129.

7. Pran Chopra *India's Second Liberation* (Delhi, Vikas, 1973), quoted in Mizanur Rehman Shelly, p. 55.
8. Jayanta Kumar Ray, *Democracy and Nationalism on Trial A Study of East Pakistan*, p. 355.
9. Eclipse of East Pakistan Chronicles of Events Since Birth of East Pakistan Till October-1963, Jyoti Sengupta, p. 44.
10. *Bangladesher dalil o Shangbadpatre Netaji Subhash*, Ratan Lal Chakrobarty, p. iii.
11. Abul Hashim, *Amaar Jibon o bibhagpurbo Bangladesher Rajnity*, p. 48.
12. *Ibid.*, p. 48.
13. *Ibid.*, p. 48.
14. Jayanta Kumar Ray, *Democracy and Nationalism on Trial a Study of East Pakistan.*
15. *Ibid.*, p. 1.
16. Jayanta Kumar Ray *Democracy and Nationalism on Trial a Study of East Pakistan* (Indian Institute of Advanced Study, Simla, 1998), p. 54.
17. 'Forum 25 April, 1970', 'Pakistan's Economic Development 1958-1969'.
18. *Ibid.*
19. *Ibid.*
20. Sunday Morning News January 17, 1960, 'Second Five-Year Plan' Economic Objectives by Mumtaz Hasan, Deputy Chairman, Planning Commission.
21. *Ibid.*, p. 4.
22. *Ibid.*, p. 4.
23. *Ibid.*, p. 4.
24. *Ibid.*, p. 4.
25. *Ibid.*, p. 4.
26. *Ibid.*, p. 4.
27. *Ibid.*, p. 4.
28. *Ibid.*, p. 4.
29. *Ibid.*, p. 4.
30. *Ibid.*, p. 4.
31. *Ibid.*, p. 4.
32. *Ibid.*, p. 4.
33. *Ibid.*, p. 4.
34. *Ibid.*, p. 4.
35. *Ibid.*, p. 4.
36. *Ibid.*, p. 4.
37. *Ibid.*, p. 4.
38. *Ibid.*, p. 4.
39. *Ibid.*, p. 4.
40. 'Morning News', Karachi, Friday, January 22, 1960, Vol. VII, No. 158.
41. *Ibid.*
42. *Ibid.*
43. *Ibid.*

44. *Ibid.*
45. *Ibid.*
46. Muntasir Mamoon, Jayanta Kumar Ray, *Civil Society in Bangladesh Resilience and Retreat*, p. 55 (Firma KLM Pvt. Ltd., 1996, Calcutta).
47. *Ibid.*
48. Ferdousi Priyobhashini, '*Anek Mrityu Dekhechi, Nary Nirjataner Katha shunechi kintu kokhono bhabini ami tar shikar hobo*'in *Ekattorer Dushaho Smriti*, edited by Shariyar Kabir.
49. Ayesha Jalal, *The State of Martial Rule*.
50. Jayanta Kumar Ray, *Democracy and Nationalism on Trial A Study of East Pakistan* (Indian Institute of Advanced Study, Simla), 1968, p. i.
51. *Ibid.*, p. 46.
52. *Ibid.*, p. 2.
53. *Ibid.*, p. 9.
54. *Ibid.*, p. i.
55. *Ibid.*, p. i.
56. Asim Roy, *Islam in South Asia A Regional Perspective* (South Asian Publishers, New Delhi) p. 1.
57. *Ibid.*, p. 1.
58. Syed Anwar Hosain, 'Islamic Fundamentalism in Bangladesh Internal Variables and External Inputs', in Rafiuddin Ahmed edited, *Religion. Nationalism and Politics in Bangladesh*, p. 138 (South Asian Publishers, New Delhi).

6

The War of Independence (1971)

With the year 1971, one lands on an ocean of troublesome time. It is very difficult to construct the history of the year from innumerable source materials, published and unpublished. The conflict between the Pakistan army group supported by the Bangladesh fundamentalists and those fighting tooth-and-nail for the liberation of the country is a wonderful phenomenon but to construct the history of the year, one has to be entangled with a huge amount of literary and documentary sources. Therefore, one has to pick-and-choose sources which may seem to be very relevant for the construction of the history of 1971. Here, some of the newspapers and published materials and books have been used for the writing of the history of 1971. One interesting aspect in this context is the abundance of oral history which may be said to be a new factor for the history of the crucial year 1971.

In the last millennium, when Bangladesh was liberated, fundamentalist forces, that had been identified with Pakistan and had opposed the very creation of Bangladesh, were on the run. By participating in the liberation struggle and by bearing more than its share of the sacrifice that was required to achieve freedom, the minority community had clearly earned the right to be treated with equality and honour in the new state that had emerged, i.e., Bangladesh. A necessary condition for this was the establishment of a secular state. That expectation was realized in 1972 when Bangladesh enshrined secularism in its constitution.

Bangladesh's tryst with Islam appears all the more surprising given its experience with Pakistan, especially the genocide that took place in the early seventies. Indeed, Pakistani officers and mullahs were supporting the Pakistani state to motivate *jawans* from West

Pakistan to carry out the massacres used religious sentiments. Thus Bangladesh's adoption of secularism was consistent with its experience with Islamic reaction in the early seventies. Yet before the decade was over, Sheikh Mujibur Rehman was dead and secularism was no longer a part of Bangladesh's Constitution. And what inevitably followed was the deterioration in the treatment of minorities.

Since the dominant segments of the indigenous elites to whom colonialism transferred power in South Asia had grown under colonial culture, though challenging it as subalterns, they did not shake off the colonial legacy, and plunged into the process of exploitation of parts of their own country, if and when possible. The relationship between East and West Pakistan viewed from this angle may form an interesting case-study of "internal colonization".

In fact the political history of Bangladesh shows that memory and oral history have an important contribution in East Pakistani freedom struggle. It continued for many years and a real description of the situation of how women were harassed and persecuted by the soldiers can be found in the writings of many radical thinkers of Bangladesh, such as Shariyar Kabir and Sukumar Biswas. They described how there was a '*ganakabar*', or mass burial of Hindu minorities in different parts of Dhaka and Chittagong. A large number of ordinary people and students had been martyrs, but those who had survived the attack of 1971 Pakistani generals, had been interviewed and interrogated by many scholars and intellectuals of independent Bangladesh. The victims were mostly poor women, who often tried to deny the stories of rape and other oppression on them. So, it is the task of the interviewee to take out words from their own mouth and learn about their poverty. This is how memory and oral history play a distinct part in the formation of nationalist history of Bangladesh.

Social history of Bangladesh can also be constructed from various historical writings by various authors, and one concrete example may be, '*Gayatri Shandhya*', three volumes written by the well-known author Selina Hossain. A socio-political history of the language movement of Bangladesh has been constructed in five volumes edited by Atiur Rehman and Lenin Azad.

When the Moghuls ruled, Burmese pirate invaded, the Mahrattas (a warrior caste for Maharashtra) came and when the British took over, they looted and robbed Bengal. Horror of such incidents created a sense of loss which seems to have entered the soul of the Bengalis. In 1970-1, Pakistani pillage was a malady for many Bangladeshis who were poverty-stricken and were struck by flood and such other diseases. Only in 1971, for a short time, Bangabandhu Sheikh Mujibur Rehman inspired the Bengali youth.

There was a growth of left-radical sentiments in Bangladesh throughout the fifties and sixties, often straying into the end of the decade, when Maulana Bhasani would lead the Bengalis to the anti-Ayub upsurge. Sheikh Mujib was in jail and yet flags of independence could be seen flying in rallies and assemblies without the Awami League leadership.

In the Kagmari conference of the Awami League, on the first days meeting of the Council on 7 February, Suhrawardy spoke with clarity on foreign policy.[1] It was here that Suhrawardy for the first time made it clear that he as Prime Minister had no obligations to his political party and that he was for the government and not for the party in the matter of state policies. He bypassed the Party issue on foreign policy by claiming 'success' on the Kashmir question at the Security Council meeting.[2]

Although the Council adopted a rule empowering the President to take disciplinary action against any member of the party violating its mandates, no action, not even in the shape of a warning, was taken against Suhrawardy or for that matter, against Sheikh Mujibur Rehman and others who ignored the firm resolutions demanding change of foreign policy and scrapping of the military pacts.

In the course of his speech, Suhrawardy adopted Maulana Bhasani's strategy and offered to resign if the Councilors did not approve of his stand. There was little difference in the politics of the nationalist and radicals during the fifties and sixties. In spite of the attempts such as successfully provoking Maulana Bhasani into resigning from the chairmanship of the Awami League on 18 March, 1957, and the formation of the National Awami Party on the 26th July of the same year, 1971 proved that these were really two complementary currents in the same liberationist struggle. One was the liberation struggle of Sheikh Mujibur Rehman and another was the pro-Chinese team of Maulana Bhasani. In 1971, both the groups had to be reckoned with by West Pakistan. Maulana Bhasani resigned from the Chairmanship and formed the National Awami Party. If we look at the socio-cultural picture, it was also a part of political phenomenon.

In 1962 Field-Marshal Ayub Khan imposed an authoritarian constitution and instituted a system of so-called, 'basic democracy'.[3] It was virtually a dictatorship under a democratic grab. The national assembly had little power, the independence of the judiciary was severely curtailed and the executive was made all powerful. The Bengalis began to feel that only through a system of parliamentary democracy based on adult franchise could they expect to get their due share in the administration of the country.

Basically, the Awami League was a constitutional political party. Its leadership was acquainted with the mechanism and practices of constitutional politics. It was not possible on its part to undertake a well-planned revolutionary programme of action.[4] For this limitation and failure the party leadership paid a heavy price. It should be noted, however, that the then Pakistan government had charged the Awami League and Sheikh Mujibur Rehman alone from launching the liberation war. This was clearly spelled out in the Pakistan government White Paper which was published during the war. In fact, the government was taking steps to try and condemn Sheikh Muji to death for the alleged crime of starting to wage the war against Pakistan. General Yahya Khan had arrogantly proclaimed: "This time Mujib will not go unpunished".[5]

In 1968, Ayub Khan argued in a speech that all regional languages should be integrated to innovate a great Pakistani language.[6] To illustrate this point, in 1968, the Academic Council of Dhaka University recommended that the Bengali language should be reformed. But in the same period (1947-71), a strong secular sentiment was taking grip of the Bengali mind. Consequently there started a struggle against Islamisation, and resistance by the civil society led to a retreat of the authorities, and this movement for the innovation of a single language for Pakistan was a failure. As a part of this resistance campaign, in July 1968, the writers' union organized a five-day function in honour of Rabindranath, Mirza Ghalib, Iqbal, Michael Madhusudhan and Qazi Nazrul. Abul Hashim delivered an important speech on this occasion, and observed that those who advocated a boycott of Rabindranath's songs on the pretext of following Islam were not only foolish but also mischievous, who understood neither Islam nor Rabindranath, and who wanted to serve a special interest by denouncing Rabindranath Tagore.

However, during the lengthy month of struggle for freedom, the Pakistani army had settled themselves in Bangladesh. The soldiers performed the worst kind of genocide on the Bengalis, both the Hindus and the Muslims, the main targets of attack being the religious minorities and Hindus.

Following is the text of statement made on 1 April, 1971, by Senator Edward M. Kennedy in the United States Senate: "President, Reports from East Pakistan tell of heavy toll being paid by the civilian population as a result of the current conflict. It is a story of indiscriminate killing, the execution of dissident political leaders and students, and thousands of civilians suffering and dying every hour of the day. It is a story of dislocation and loss of home. It is a story of little food and water. And coming in the aftermath of tragedy by natural disaster, the current violence and total disruption of government services in East Pakistan is compounding to an already difficult situation. It threatens near famine for millions and the spread of epidemics and disease.[7] ..."

"Inevitably, the situation of civilians in East Pakistan is taking second place to the political issues at state—and to the interest of those who have much to lose, or to gain, by the outcome of the battle. But the people of Dhaka, of Chittagong, and of the villages and towns throughout the area also have interests. For many, apparently, it is mere survival."[8]

During the crisis in 1971, the members of religious political parties like Jamaat-e-Islami, Muslim League, Nizam-e-Islami and others, in the name of preserving Islam and maintaining the integrity of Pakistan, pressed the Pakistani army to perform genocide, violence on women and dacoities and they themselves actively participated in the process.

Immediately after the crackdown of the Pakistan armed forces, on the 26 March, 1971, the Islamic parties and supporters of Pakistan tried to establish close link with the Pakistan authorities. As a part of this plan, Peace Committees (under the shadow of the name, they were extremely militant) were formed on the 9 April. Jamaat-e-Islami and some Ulemas stood on the core of the committees, with the

Muslim League, Nizam-e-Islami and *Krishak Sramik* Party joining them. From the Ulemas to the peasants, different groups came together.

The committee opened liaison offices in various parts of Dhaka city after April 1971, in the offices of '*Jamaat-e-Islami*'. In association with this move at the center, local branches and students organizations under their influence formed action groups to counter the guerilla attacks and execute the supporters of the liberation struggle. In November 1971, '*Al Badr*' was born. The main groups were: 1. Razakars: Abbas Ali Khan started organizing this group in Bogra; 2. *Al Badar*: (*Islami Chhatra Sangha*), the student wing of the Muslim League; 3. *Al Shams*, responsible for massacre of students in Chittagong. Siddiq Saliq says that, these patriotic elements were organized into two groups.[9] The elderly and prominent among them formed Peace Committees, while the young and able-bodied were recruited as *Razakars* (volunteers). The Committees were formed in Dhaka and in the rural areas as well, and they served as a useful link between the army and the local people. At the same time, they earned the wrath of the rebels and 250 of them were killed, wounded or kidnapped.

Razakars were raised to augment the strength of the West Pakistani troops and to give a sense of participation in the local population. Their manpower rose to nearly 50,000 as against a target of 1,00,000. In September a political delegation from West Pakistan complained to General A.K. Niazi that he had raised an army of *Jamaat-e-Islami* nominees.

The *Al-Badr* and *Al-Shams* groups were a dedicated lot, keen to help the army. They worked and suffered hard. About 5000 of them or their dependents suffered at the hands of the Mukti Bahini for the crime of co-operation. Some of them displayed a sense of sacrifice comparable to the best troops of the world.

In terms of training and weapon, however, the Razakars were no match for the Mukti Bahini. That may be one of the reasons for the reason of the failure of West Pakistani troops. Strategically as well, the East Pakistani troops had the benefit of distance between the two provinces, and the West Pakistani fighter planes were long outdated and old-fashioned.

Sukumar Biswas in his article, '*Chattagramer Badhyabhumi: Pahartalir mati khurle ekhono kuri hazar Bangalir mathar khuli paowa jabe*', has elaborated, after making a visit to Chittagong, that the Pakistani generals had killed at least more than 20 Bengalis. The number of murdered Bengalis should be at least three lakh. If the city and the suburbs are excavated, then at least 20 to 25 thousand skulls of Bengalis may be discovered in areas like mango grove, wireless colony, Sher Shah Colony and Fayez Lake.[10] Their intellectual activities were against the population in general.

The three groups having organized the executive wing of the Peace Committee, co-operated with the Pakistani army, and led terrorist actions against the supporters of the liberation, both in urban and rural areas. No less than 5000 execution yards were their creations, to kill the sympathisers of the liberation struggle. One of the key figures at this juncture of history of Bangladesh was Golam Azam, who, in November 1971, went from Lahore to East Pakistan to join a meeting of the central committee of the '*Jamaat-e-Islami*'. So, he appealed to all Pakistanis to forget their political affiliations and to unite against the Bangladesh freedom movement.

I had the opportunity to go to Dhaka with my mother and a personal meeting with Golam Azam was arranged. I found that the former Ameer of 'Jamaat-e-Islami' was extremely educated, well-mannered, polite and had certain beliefs in the theory of Islam. He distributed many pamphlets of his party, amongst which, one particular pamphlet was an interview of Golam Azam by the BBC, '*Mediar Mukhomukhi Golam Azam*'. He described the theory of Islam and what mission it had for the general public, of keeping peace and harmony throughout the world. He was well-mannered and polite towards the two Hindu women.

There has been a great deal of controversy on the different parties, personalities and political camps, on the role of politics in the freedom movement of Bangladesh. Golam Azam in his above-mentioned interview pointed out that, 'Jamaat-e-Islami' and other Muslim parties did not play an active part in the freedom movement, as it was basically an intrusion by the Indian government. He further said that even Sheikh Mujibur Rehman, the leader of Awami League, did not want such freedom taken from the hands of India. The opinion of the leftist parties in Bangladesh is quite different. Sukumar Biswas in his book, *Bangladesher muktiyuddhe CPIM o ganashakti* (February 2001), points out that, seven crore Bengalis in East Pakistan made their protest against the cruelty and extortion of West Pakistanis. The freedom movement was organized in the year 1971, and an independent state was created, but the storm of protest started from the time of the language movement in 1952. If the old Muslim families were to succeed in transforming their social-pre-eminence into political power, it was clear that the United Muslim Party would have to win a share of the rural voters.

The unreasonable demand that Pakistan made on India was that India should stop sending, "infiltrators in to Pakistan". It was known to everyone that India did not send the so-called "infiltrators" into Pakistan, nor did they need to send them. In Bangladesh guerilla warfare was being directed by the *Mukti Bahini* of Bangladesh, that is, the people's forces. The retaliatory action by the Mukti Bahini was proving too much for Pakistan. Now they wanted that India should resist the *Mukti Bahini* on Pakistan's behalf. There was a limit to arrogance. But the military regime had lost all sense of propriety. Though the people and government of the People's Republic of Bangladesh were grateful to the Indian government for giving shelter to and maintaining 90 million refugees, the Bangladesh government and *Mukti Bahini* were by no means obliged to follow India's will and desire on the question of national independence; nor did India have any involvement with the issue.

The Communist Party of India had its own position in the fiery situation in Bengal from March, 1971, and supported the deprived general population in the great freedom movement. Sukumar Biswas in his book has pointed out how the daily struggle of the ordinary people in East Pakistan and the extortion by West Pakistani rulers was continuously focused specially through '*Ganashakti*'.[11] The Marxist Communist Party played an important role in organizing pubic opinion in favour of the struggling masses, everywhere in India, including West Bengal.

On 27 March, a student's strike was conducted in West Bengal, in support of the struggling student-masses in Bangladesh. On the very same day, a twelve hours strike was called in Agartala, in support of the struggling masses in Bangladesh. In different places in West Bengal, all working classes in the factories called 'tool down strike', for one hour.

In this context, a book, *Independence of Bangladesh In 266 Days*

History and Documentary Evidence, written by freedom fighter Muhammad Nurul Quadir, may be used properly. He was the Press-Reporter-cum-Photographer, the Daily *Ittefaq*, Rajshahi University, 1961; Joint Secretary, Rajshahi Press Club, 1962; Joint Editor, Rajshahi University Magazine etc. The historic proposal of the Dhaka Bar Association dated 22 February, 1965 for conducting all business in courts and offices in Bengali language, adopted unanimously, was tabled by him. He was elected a Basic Democrated Member from South Kamalpur, Dhaka. He was the Chairman, Ward Committee, and was elected Secretary-General of East Pakistan Basic Democrat Association, 1965. He was President, Dilkhusha Union Awami League (1965-72).

He was the first to resign in East Pakistan from the post of the Chairman of the Ward Committee and Basic Democrat Member in protest against the policies of Field Marshall Mohammed Ayub Khan, President of Pakistan and as a result almost all the Basic Democrat Members resigned. As such the system of Basic Democracy failed.

During the War of independence of Bangladesh, on 14 July, 1971, a movie interview of Advocate Muhammad Nurul Qadir was filmed in the studio of Film Division, Bombay, and exhibited in the Cinema House of India. Again, it was Sunday, 7 March, 1971, *Bangabandhu* (Friend of Bengal) Sheikh Mujibur Rehman, the father of the nation, stood tall and erect, his head held high on the huge Dias of what was then the Racecourse ground of Dhaka. From this position he proclaimed the independence of Bangladesh indirectly in a ringing voice before a mammoth public meeting (human sea) and a large number of local and foreign newsmen. He mentioned the formation of the interim government.

Mujib's announcement of the Six-Point Programme in February 1966 almost synchronized with the retributive action by the Ayub regime. The Sheikh along with his close lieutenants was put behind the bars in April 1966. In January 1968 the Government of East Pakistan leveled a trumped-up charge of having entered into a conspiracy with "the Indian agents" to bring about the secession of East Bengal from Pakistan against Sheikh Mujib and several senior officers of the civil service and the armed forces.[12] The so-called Agartala conspiracy case in which they were implicated instantly turned out to be the symbol of Bengali nationalism. Throughout the late 60s massive anti-government demonstrations sent the whole of East Bengal into convulsions. In the meanwhile, the government's failure to put forth enough evidence in the case against the Sheikh and others led to their unconditional release from jail on 22 February 1969.

From that historic moment onwards the Sheikh started riding remarkable successes one after another. Around the same time also West Pakistan was constantly rocked by movements for restoration of a democratic political process. In the face of such popular rage in both the wings of Pakistan, President Ayub, who had been ailing from mid-1968, was compelled to hand over power to his Commander-in-Chief of the army, General Yahya Khan on 25 March 1969.

It was an irony of history that the task of presiding over Pakistan's disintegration fell on General Yahya Khan. Immediately after taking over power from Ayub, President Yahya Khan declared that his interim government's main objective was to create "conditions conducive to the establishment of a constitutional government." The Legal Framework Order (LFO) promulgated by the President on 30 March 1970 set the ball rolling for the general elections slated for October 1970. The LFO provided for a federal structure for Pakistan with maximum provincial autonomy, framed electoral rules for the National Assembly, and set the stage for popular participation on the basis of Universal franchise etc.

While making these political concessions, President Yahya and his political and military advisers were apparently encouraged by the wishful thinking that because of the disparate nature of Pakistan's political parties and groups no stable government would be formed by the political parties after the general elections and the resulting political imbroglio would help the ruling clique to legitimize military rule in the country.

Things, however, moved in a different direction and stunned the Yahya regime as the results of the postponed national elections (subsequently held on 7 December 1970) started pouring in. Sheikh Mujib's Awami League scored a landslide victory in both the National Assembly and the Provincial Assembly. Fighting the elections as "a referendum on the autonomy issue", the Awami League captured as many as 167 seats out of 169 seats reserved for East Pakistan in the National Assembly and 298 seats (including ten seats reserved for women) out of a total of 310 seats in the Provincial Assembly. In

West Pakistan, on the other hand, Z.A. Bhutto's Pakistan People's Party could win only 81 seats out of the 144 seats reserved for the West in the National Assembly.

The Awami League's overwhelming victory in the first ever national elections sent shock waves of alarm into the citadel of the military-bureaucratic ruling clique in Islamabad. The situation turned out to be all the more uncomfortable for the power elite when Mujib blared in a victory rally on 19 December 1970 that he warmly thanked the people for having given a historic verdict in favour of their six-point programme. They pledged to implement this verdict.[13]

On 16 February 1971 Bhutto announced that the PPP would boycott the National Assembly's inaugural session to be held on 3 March 1971 unless the Sheikh modified his programme for regional autonomy. On 28 February he demanded postponement of the National Assembly session "to facilitate fresh talks" between the PPP and the Awami League. That Bhutto had been working towards a political showdown with Mujib at the behest of President Yahya and his coterie of advisers became clear when the President rushed to announce on 1 March that he was putting off the inauguration of the National Assembly to allow the two contending leaders of both the wings to arrive at a consensus.

With the ominous move President Yahya seemed to have crossed the Rubicon, which spelled disaster both for himself and the whole of Pakistan. Recounting "the saga of the escalating domestic crisis" facing Yahya Khan, an observer wrote, "the gathering storm in East Pakistan loomed ominously over the horizon. Yahya Khan, whose achievements even as a military leader were questionable, was ill-equipped to deal with the complexity of the issues that were being raised. His circle of adviser was narrowing and the callibre of advice was uneven."[14]

Both Mujib and Bhutto were taking irreversible stances towards political impasse. Of the two leading figures of the Pakistani politics, Mujib's total lack of interest in becoming the leader of United Pakistan was paralleled by Bhutto's "equally unexpected insistence not to settle for the second highest position" in Pakistan leadership.[15]

Whosoever might have been responsible for the constitutional deadlock in the wake of the general election in Pakistan and for its impending doom, the indefinite postponement of the National Assembly's inaugural session by Yahya Khan convinced the people of East Pakistan that the West Pakistan ruling clique would not transfer power to the Awami League.

Understanding the restive mood of the Bengalis, Sheikh Mujib gave a call for a non-cooperation movement from 1 March to 25 March, 1971. People from all walks of life spontaneously responded to the call and life in East Pakistan was brought to a standstill. In order to terrorise the Bengalis at this stage Yahya Khan appointed Lt. General Tikka Khan, an army officer infamous for his ruthlessness and saddist temperament, as the Governor of East Pakistan. At this critical situation both Mujib and Yahya Khan were looking for a vital breathing space to prepare for the final showdown.[16] The Sheikh, on his part, was still not serious about seceding from Pakistan.

The main problem was to isolate the rebels from the innocent people. They usually mixed like fish in water. It was suggested to General Tikka Khan that the 3-km border belt be depopulated so that the troops could shoot all suspects in the area. General Tikka Khan, however, turned down the suggestion. He felt that it would aggravate the rehabilitation problem and he was already occupied with the resettlement of refugees returning from India in response to the general amnesty announced on 4 September.

So the rebels and their hosts continued to mix. It was difficult to distinguish one from the other as all of them looked alike. A rebel carrying a sten gun under his arm could, in emergency, throw his weapon in the field and start working like an innocent farmer. On the other hand, a report was received in Rajshahi that rebels had entered the Rohanpur area and were forcing the people to give them food, money and shelter. A group of soldiers searched the area but found no one except three farmers working in the field. This kind of brilliant strategy of finding hide-outs may be the causality for the defeat of Pakistani army in the warfare.

President Yahya Khan went on a long mental holiday after ordering the army crackdown on 25 March. Apparently he lost all interest in East Pakistan and took no advantage of the time bought by his troops with their sweat etc. Several explanations have been forwarded for Yahya's inaction, of which, particular attention may be given to that of General G.W. Chowdhury.[17] General Chowdhury gave the impression that Yahya Khan, a delicate soul, was shocked at the barbarity of his troops.[18]

In eight months of protracted guerilla warfare in 1971, President Yahya Khan, one of the most misunderstood figures in the history of Pakistan, took only two decisions: the replacement of Governor Tikka Khan and the grant of a general amnesty to the rebels. He exercised his political discretion only after repeated suggestions.

Zulfiqar Ali Bhutto refused to participate in the discussions to frame the new constitution—led to the continuation of the martial law and the eventual political and military confrontation between East and West Pakistan, which precipitated civil war and the country's dismemberment in December 1971. The imposition of martial law failed to curb domestic unrest, and civil war between East and West Pakistan broke out in 1971. The defeat of Pakistan's army and the ultimate success of Bangladesh caused him to resign late in 1971.

As mentioned earlier, the rise of *Bangabandhu* Sheikh Mujibur Rehman has been traced in India and Bangladesh, and he was a student-leader of the Awami League. A visit to his residence at *Dhanmondi* in Dhaka, where he was assassinated later, illustrates the life of the middle-class politician who was basically honest and brave. He risked his life for the sake of independence of Bangladesh, but was killed by pro-Pakistani forces on 15 August, 1975.

7 March should have been fixed as the Independence Day of Bangladesh, rather than 26 March, since the announcements made on the Independent (*Swadhin*) Bangladesh Radio on 26th and 27th March were simply repetitions of the Declaration of Independence made on 7th March, 1971.

Equipped with all modern weapons, the West Pakistan army had surrounded Rajarbagh Police Lines, Police Head Quarters, Police Barracks, the headquarters of the East Pakistan Rifles at Peelkhana, the army cantonment there, several students' residential halls at Dhaka University and a number of slum areas. They had thereafter begun to bombard all those areas simultaneously. The deafening explosions were illuminating the night sky of 25 March, 1971.

No one would ever know exactly how many people were killed and wounded that night. There can be few such examples of such an unprovoked, cowardly and barbaric attack made by a modern army of a civilized country on its own unarmed, innocent people. Bangabandhu had delivered his speech on 7th March. On that day Major Zia, in his grave and vibrant voice, announced the independence of Bangladesh on behalf of Sheikh Mujibur Rehman from the makeshift broadcasting center at Kalurghat in Chittagong set up by the freedom-fighters.

In the address given by Tajuddin Ahmed, Prime Minister, on behalf of the government of Bangladesh, headed by Sheikh Mujibur Rehman, broadcast by Swadhin Bangladesh Betar Kendra, 1971, it was said that a mighty army was being formed around the nucleus of the professional soldiers from the Bangladesh Regiment and East Pakistan Rifles (E.P.R.) who had rallied to the cause of the liberation struggle. These have been joined by the police, Ansars and Mujahids. At that time, thousands of Awami League and other volunteers were being trained into a fighting force ready to use the captured weapons from the defeated West Pakistani mercenaries and fresh arms were being purchased from funds collected by the Bangladeshi brothers overseas. An effort was made to build up public opinion in favour of the freedom fighters of East Pakistan.

Tajuddin Ahmed further pointed out that, the military part of the struggle was however only one aspect of the war. The war for survival was transmitted within Bangladesh. The U.S.S.R. and India had taken notice of the genocide, and the U.S.S.R. had urged Pakistan to desist from its acts of repression. Even Britain had taken cognizance of the configuration, whilst Ceylon and Burma had responded to world opinion by refusing refueling rights to Pakistani planes carrying their cargo of death to Dhaka.

Whilst there was still talk in some countries of this being an internal affair of Pakistan, it was becoming evident that the massacre of 75 million people and the attempt to suppress their struggle for freedom was now an international issue of major dimension which threatened the conscience as much as the peace of the region. The government of Bangladesh had already used the services of patriotic Bengalis abroad to draw attention to the notice of the world.

Prime Minister Tajuddin Ahmed said that at 10 am on April 15, a secret emergency meeting was being held at the MLA Hostel in Calcutta. A group of people were found discussing what measures that to be taken to win over world opinion in favour of Bangladesh during the liberation war.[19] Writer Mizanur Rehman Chowdhury listened with great attention to the important speeches delivered by the leaders and noted down the salient points. He informed the Awami

League leaders that after having a discussion on those points with Prime Minister Tajuddin Ahmed, everyone would again meet at the MLA hostel at 10 a.m. on 18 April, 1971. Later on, all would join in a separate session in another venue to discuss all those points in detail and reach a final decision.

Writer Azizur Rehman Mullick and many others in their respective autobiographies like, '*Amar Ekattor*', explains that not only in India, but in other foreign countries as well, there was a large attempt to gather public opinion in favour of the independence movement of 1971. Several newspapers, beginning with '*Anandabazar Patrika*', used to waive public pressure in favour of the Awami League and other parties.

Freedom fighter Muhammad Nurul Qadir came to know from Justice S.A. Masud that there has been an organization named 'India-Pakistan Friendship Society' in Kolkata since independence in 1947. Sher-e-Bangla A.K. Fazlul Huq had sent a letter of congratulation to that organization. The name of the organisation has been changed to '*Bharat*-Bangladesh Friendship Society'. He was the President of that organization and the Vice-Presidents were: Bhupesh Gupta, MP; Ajit Kumar Dutta, Advocate; Amar Chakrobarty, Advocate and Arun Mukhopadhyay. The main function of the *Bharat*-Bangladesh Friendship Society was to obtain immediate recognition of independent Bangladesh from all countries including India and to create world opinion in order that the West Pakistan military regime would be compelled to stop genocide in Bangladesh immediately.

Saturday, 17 April, 1971, was a very important day in the history of Bangladesh, as it was marked by the proclamation of Bangladesh's independence and the swearing in, openly, of the first cabinet of the Bangladesh Government in the liberated area of Mujibnagar before a gathering of over a hundred foreign and local journalists, press photographers, radio and TV people. Prime Minister Tajuddin Ahmed renamed the *Ambagan* (Mango grove) in Bhaberpara Baidyanathtala of Meherpur under Kushtia district as '*Mujibnagar*'—and made it the temporary capital of Bangladesh. Prime Minister Tajuddin Ahmed, acting President Syed Nazrul Islam, and other leaders reached Mujibnagar by 8a.m. in the morning. Some chairs, most of them armless, were brought for the leaders from the nearby villages.

It took about four hours for the procession of vehicles carrying the journalists from Calcutta Press Club to reach the historic *Ambagan* (Mango Grove) in Mujibnagar. At the meeting site, high over the dais, were a large number of mahogany trees. The shadow of a sky covered with wispy clouds fell on the surrounding landscape. It was an atmosphere of ineffable beauty and delight.

Almost two hundred years after 23rd June, 1757, when the sun of independence of Bengal, Bihar and Orissa had eclipsed (Battle of Plassey), a new sun of sovereign independent Bangladesh rose on 17th April, 1971, in the sky of Meherpur, once part of that ancient district of Nadia.

In the beginning, the local *Moulana* (religious functionary), wearing a white *tupi* (cap), checked *lungi* and white shirt inaugurated the occasion by reciting from the Holy Quran. After hoisting the National Flag of independent Bangladesh and inspecting the guard of honour presented by the newly constituted Armed Forces, the acting President Syed Nazrul Islam accompanied by Tajuddin Ahmed, the Commander-in-Chief of the Freedom Fighters Col. Mohammed Ataul Ghani Osmany, Foreign and Law Minister Khondkar Moshtaq Ahmed, Home, Relief and Rehabilitation Minister A.H.M. Quamruzzaman, and Finance Minister Captain M. Mansur Ali mounted the meeting platform.

The volunteers showered them with flowers. Four boys rendered the national anthem, '*Amar sonar Bangla ami tomay bhalobashi ...*'to the accompaniment of a harmonium and the beating of drums. It was heavenly music and all were welcome by emotion and everyone's eyes were full of tears of joy. All the members of the audience stood up to show their respect. The leaders wore white Punjabi and payajamas. Only the Foreign Minister wore deep grey long coat, pants and a *Tupi* (cap). The function was conducted by Abdul Mannan who was in charge of the information, publicity and radio on behalf of the Prime Minister. The Chief Whip of the Awami League, Professor Mohammed Yusuf Ali read the Proclamation of Independence and conducted the function amidst repeated claps and slogans affirming support.

As per advice of the Prime Minister Tajuddin Ahmed three ministers were appointed. The acting President Syed Nazrul Islam delivered high-spirited speech. On two occasions during the speech he spoke in English, when he was seeking sympathy, help and recognition from the world community for the newly independent state. He requested everyone present, particularly the foreign journalists, to convey his appeal to all the countries of the world, big and small, including Afro-Asian countries.

He praised all the freedom-fighters of the country—students, youths, armed forces, EPR, police, East Bengal Regiment, Ansar and Mujahid—for their bravery. After the oath-taking ceremony, Prime Minister Tajuddin Ahmed read an eight-page statement. In the statement he mentioned that Yahya Khan, by carrying out genocide, had in fact dug the grave of Pakistan. He announced with deep conviction that the world's eighth most populous country, Bangladesh, would take its place amongst the community of nations in the world. All present were overwhelmed with the moving speech of Prime Minister Tajuddin Ahmed.

In the meantime, facts may be ascertained about the exodus to present West Bengal and the border areas. This exodus was the result of widespread minority killings in Rajshahi and Pabna districts in 1962 and in Dhaka and other areas in 1964-5. A Canadian correspondent from Montreal gave a truthful account of the programme of 1964-5, which the United States and the Pakistan government wanted to hide by a conspiracy of silence.

Hundreds of wounded men and women were brought in open trucks to the poorly staffed hospitals of Dhaka. Foreign doctors offered their services to these hospitals, but the Pakistani doctors turned down the offer. An indirect result of the refugee thrust was development of small colonies in and around Calcutta.

The widely circulated English daily *Blitz* published from Bombay, India, on its issue of the 10th of April, 1971, printed a map, which was sent from the war front of Bangladesh. That map showed areas in Bangladesh that were being controlled by the West Pakistani military and also areas controlled by the Bangladesh freedom fighters. The map clearly demarcated the two sections. Next came in the map, where the forces were engaged in intensive struggle for control and the potential future flashpoints. According to that map, the West Pakistan army was controlling the Dhaka and Jessore cantonment areas, Rangpur, Chittagong, Bhola, Noakhali town and Chalna port whereas Comilla, Rajshahi, Dinajpur, Chittagong Hill Tracts, Mymensingh, Kushtia, Barisal and other frontier areas, including

Jessore, were under the control of the Mukti Bahini (freedom fighters). The West Pakistan army and the Mukti Bahini, on the other hand, were locked in serious battles in Khulna, Bogra. The war, it seemed that, could flare up any time in Dinajpur, Rajshahi, Rangamati, Mymensingh and some parts of Sylhet.

Even in Calcutta, news came in the daily *Jugantar* of Calcutta carrying out a banner heading which was as follows: The emergence of the Republic of Bangladesh amidst the slogan, '*Joy Bangla*'. Therefore, on Sunday, the 18th April 1971, the Awami League leaders again met at 10 am in the dining hall of MLA hostel Calcutta. The Acting General Secretary of the Awami League, Mizanur Rahman Chowdhury, took everyone to another place to maintain secrecy.

In Calcutta, what was happening in Dhaka had also an important repercussion. All relevant issues were discussed at length in the meeting and a unanimous decision was taken to the effect that the Awami League leaders would visit different refugee camps situated in the border areas and extend all possible help to ensure accommodation, safety and supply of relief to the refugees. It was also decided for further improving the administration and overall condition of the transit camps and also to make arrangements for appropriate and necessary training for the Freedom Fighters for future activities.

Thereafter followed a unique incident. On 18 April, 1971, Pakistan's Deputy High Commissioner in Kolkata M. Hossain Ali, who had served Pakistan Foreign Service for 22 years, renounced his loyalty to Pakistan and declared allegiance to Bangladesh. Along with him First General Secretary Rafiqul Alam Chowdhury, Third Secretaries Anwarul Karim Chowdhury and Kazi Nazrul Islam and many others sowed their allegiance to the Bangladesh government. During that critical phase of liberation war the expression of loyalty to Bangladesh government as shown by M. Hossain Ali and his colleagues, was undoubtedly an instance of extraordinary courage and a historic event. Later, many Bengali diplomats in other countries followed their example and expressed their allegiance to Bangladesh.

On 18 April, 1971, the Chief of the Bangladesh Mission, M. Hossain Ali, brought down India's national flag from the High Commission Office and hoisted the national flag of independent Bangladesh at the 'Bangladesh Mission' in front of many local and foreign journalists and press photographers. That was a moment of joy and historic significance. The Bangladesh Mission situated at 9 Circus Avenue, Calcutta, ultimately turned into a hub of diplomatic activities in support of the liberation war of Bangladesh. M. Hossain Ali read out his four-page statement before a large number of foreign and local journalists. In that statement he dwelt at length on the reasons why after 22 years of diplomatic assignments with Pakistan's Foreign Service, he had been compelled to opt for Bangladesh. Next day all newspapers, TV and radio broadcast all over the world carried this story.

The ravages of nature, political violence, and corruption—all conceal the fact that Bangladesh was still in the grip of a continuing and indeed undeclared civil war, the unfinished task of its creation in 1971. But after 1971, (as Charles Dickens points out in his book, *The Tale of Two Cities*, "it was the best of times, it was the worst of times"). Only the Soviet bloc and Australia recognized Bangladesh.

13 April, 1971, Prime Minister Chow En Lai of China sent a message to Pakistan' President General Yahya Khan declaring that, "Should India dare launch aggression, the government and people of China would firmly support the government and people of Pakistan in their just struggle to safeguard their sovereignty and national independence". The reaction of the USSR was quite different. A newspaper carried a story which said that Podgorny, the President of the USSR, wrote a letter to Pakistan's President General Yahya Khan urging him to "take up steps to stop bloodshed in East Pakistan" and "Stop repression on the people of East Pakistan and look for a peaceful way of political dialogue". In that letter President Podgormy further urged General Yahya Khan, "Soviet Union is very anxious about the arrest of Sheikh Mujibur Rehman and other political leaders who received overwhelming support from the people of East Pakistan during the recent general election."

From March 1971, the Marxist Communist Party of India supported the deprived common people of Bengal in their struggle for independence. At one end, they gave support to the patriotic ordinary people of East Bengal through the '*Ganashakti*' and at another end, a party representative said, 'In West Bengal also, there is a strong struggle to restore democracy in the face of the police and the military'.[20]

There was the news of disruption in East Bengal on 5 March, on 6 March it was mentioned that, 'public revolt is continuing, Yahya Khan has been forced to give instruction for the removal of the army from Dhaka, and in the newspaper of 7 March, '*Ganashakti*' categorically showed that Yahya Khan has been forced to summon the National Convention meeting on 25 March.[21] Quoting PTI and UNI sources, a report in '*Ganashakti*', showed that, Mujibur Rehman is making an appeal to 'the humanist demands of the seven and a half crore East Bengalis and they should be given a patient hearing'.[22] The reports and headings published in '*Ganashakti*' ', played an important part in creating public opinion in the movement in East Bengal.

The issue of 7 May discussed the miserable condition of the refugees. The reporter of '*Ganashakti*', severely criticized Indian government: 'Kolkata May 7: If an inspection is made over the refugee camps in Bangaon frontier, then it can be proved that there is much realistic difference in the campaigns of bourgeois newspapers or the India government, West Bengal government or *Aakaashbani* correspondents. On 29 April, the Migrant committee in totality and a few representatives like Suhrid Mallick Chowdhury M.P., Prankrishna Chakrobarty, and such other leaders went to inspect different camps like Petropol, Gyarapeta, and Bagda etc. These camps had almost 40 thousand refugees.[23]

A statistical account of refugee influx has been narrated by Prafulla Kumar Chakrobarty in his book, *The Marginal Men*. There was an upsurge of Bangladeshi people to Calcutta, out of right and tension. Even earlier, the introduction of passports for travel from Pakistan to India on October 1952, started a new exodus.

After the swearing-in-ceremony of the ministerial cabinet of the (Mujibnagar) government in the liberated area at Meherpur on 17th April 1971, acting President Syed Nurul Islam, Prime Minister Tajuddin Ahmed, Foreign Minister Khondaker Mushtaq Ahmed, Home, Relief and Rehabilitation Minister Quamuruzzaman and Finance Minister M. Mansur Ali first stayed for a few days at House No. 13, Lord Sinha Street, for the sake of security. When the news got around that they were staying at that location, they again shifted their address, for security reasons, to another house on Ballygunge Circular Road. As the interim government had been formed, they had to fly away and took shelter in Calcutta. Later, when the studio of Swadhin Bangla Betar Kendra (radio centre of independent Bangla) was established in that house on Ballygunge Circular Road, the members of the cabinet of Mujibnagar government lived in a number of flats of the eight storied building owned by Asutosh Ghosh, situated at 62 CIT Road, Calcutta. They were constantly changing their residential places.

During this time, the camp office of the Mujibnagar government was established at the house on 8, Theatre Road, Calcutta. Thus Calcutta seemed to become a part of freedom fighting movement Prime Minister Tajuddin Ahmed made arrangements for his office and living quarters in two small rooms at the corner of this house. That same place housed the temporary secretariat of the Mujibnagar government and the camp office of the Commander-in-Chief of the Freedom fighters, Col. Ataul Ghani Osmany. Over the entire period of the liberation war, Prime Minister Tajuddin Ahmed used to work day and night in that temporary secretariat as his office of the Mujibnagar government. He had both the meals of a day cooked from a mess. According to Advocate Mohammed Nurul Qadir, words fail to describe the untold hardship and inhuman workload that he had to put up with during the nine long months of liberation war.

Bangladesh Prime Minister Tajuddin Ahmed took two very important decisions that greatly helped the administration of the Mujibnagar government in exile, to tackle the situation in wartime. The Prime Minister's first remarkable task was to employ a number of efficient people as secretaries. Thus Nurul Quader Khan was appointed as Establishment Secretary, Khindoker Asaduzzaman as Finance Secretary, Abdus Samad as Defence Secretary and Hossain Towfiq Imam as Cabinet Secretary. He distributed important portfolios to competent persons. The second important work of the Prime Minister was to divide Bangladesh into 11 political zones theoretically and appoint 11 persons who were loyal to the policy of the Awami League, particularly to the policy of the Prime Minister, as zonal chairman or chiefs (political leaders). In addition, 11 other persons were appointed as administrators of 11 zones. The 11zone chairmen were given the responsibility of ensuring that only such youths as were imbued with the ideology of the Awami League would be able to receive training as freedom fighters. The zone chairmen were able to discharge their responsibilities secretly, flawlessly and faithfully. All this was taking place in Calcutta. As a result, the entire army of freedom fighters remained especially loyal to Prime Minister Tajuddin Ahmed. In Dhaka, things were given a grim picture.

The War Heroine Project received unanimous international support at the Asia-Pacific Congress of the Junior Chamber International held at Manila, Phillipines in 1973. In the earlier part of 1971, the government of Mujibnagar divided Bangladesh into 11 sectors and appointed 11 commanders. Those sector commanders were given charge of their respective areas. As they had the full power to take immediate decision about the conduct of war in the respective sectors to meet contingencies arising in specific situations, the local strategies of war depended on peculiarities of particular sectors. But one aspect was consistent everywhere—the freedom loving daredevil youths of Bangladesh staked their lives for the liberation of their motherland.

Many foreign journalists and TV camera crew were then engaged in collecting news from different battlefields and sending such news from newspapers and radio and television broadcasts. The frontier regions were crowded with refugee camps. Millions of refugees took shelter in those camps. The newspapers of almost all the countries of the world published reports and stories on the difficult situation that those refugees were facing. As a result many humanitarian organizations from abroad including the Red Cross sent through Indian government huge amount of relief material and money for those refugees.

The *'Swadhin Bangla Betar Kendra'* played an extraordinary role during the War of Liberation. They were sending news and information on war throughout the world. Of the programmes the most popular was the satirical *Charam Patra* (Ultimatum) broadcast by the *Swadhin Bangla Betar Kendra*. M.R. Akhter (Mukul) used to prepare and read the programme script. Rich in the dialect spoken by the original inhabitants of Dhaka city (*Dhakaiya*), *Charam Patra* became popular even among the people of West Bengal.

Another aspect of the freedom struggle was the attempt of the Muslim intellectuals to organize the intelligentsia in favour of the freedom movement, in this transition period. The Dhaka intellectuals tried to gather themselves in Calcutta, and this matter has been focused repeatedly in the contemporary 'New York Times' newspaper. To counter this propaganda the programme, 'In the light of Islam' was serialized by *Swadhin Bangla Betar Kendra* at this time in 1971.

Syed Ali Ahsan (ex-Minister and ex-Vice-Chancellor of Jahangirnagar University) reached Calcutta from Chittagong University through Agartala. During the conversation with freedom fighter advocate Muhammad Nurul Qadir, he expressed his keen desire to prepare and read commentaries written in the light of Islam on following topics from Swadhin Bangla Betar Kendra: 1. Democracy, 2. Humanity, 3. Homicide, 4. *Jehad* (Holy War), 5. Deceit in the name of Islam, 6. Treachery, 7. Creating communal disharmony.[24]

During the same time Hasan Zaman had been reading commentaries from the Radio and TV controlled by Pakistan from Dhaka on topics such as, "why Pakistan is on the side of Islam and why liberation war is anti-Islamic".[25] The commentaries were widely acclaimed by the Muslim audience both within Bangladesh and in West Bengal and went a long way in dispelling doubt and suspicion about the liberation war of Bangladesh among Bengali Muslims, of Indian origin in particular. In the meantime, "Bangladesh Liberation Council of the Intelligentsia" was formed. The Vice Chancellor of Chittagong University Abdur Rehman Mallick (later minister and ambassador) became its President.

Zaihar Raihan produced a major film called "Stop Genocide" in 1971. Made with the objective of stopping carnage in Bangladesh the film had a great impact internationally. Apart from his other works, Zaihar Rahman's name will remain inscribed in golden letters in the history of Bangladesh's war of liberation. Zaihar Raihan's other immortal creations (films) are "*Jiban theke Neya*" (Taken From Life), "*Let there be Light*", "State is Born", "*Kokhono Asheni*" etc.

Upon returning to Dhaka immediately after independence, Zaihar Raihan, acting on an unconfirmed report that his elder brother, renowned journalist and writer Shahidullah Kaiser {father of Shomi Kaiser, leader of Projonmo '71 (Generation '71) noted film and TV star} was imprisoned somewhere in Mirpur, Dhaka rushed there on January 30, 1972 in a bid to rescue him but disappeared forever mysteriously.

Zaihar Raihan was a very active and popular leader and General Secretary of the "*Bangladesh Liberation Council of the Intelligentsia*" during the Liberation War. Though nearly all reputed intellectuals of Bangladesh are members of that organization none of them during the last 32 years have done anything substantial to solve the puzzle of Zahir Raihan's disappearance except raising storm in a tea cup or delivering speeches at meetings standing before the microphone.

Many believe that Zahir Khan in the course of his missions with a movie camera during the Liberation War might have taken shots of something too revealing, for some that made him the target of killers who after independence, devised the plot of luring him to Mirpur to rescue his elder brother—undoubtedly the most vulnerable issue to draw unqualified response from the victim.

21 April, 1971, was a memorable day in the history of Bangladesh. On that day the octogenarian leader Maulana Abdul Hamid Khan Bhasani sent 13 telegrams and letters to the leaders of 13 countries of the world in a bid to save 75 million unarmed Bengalees from the barbaric attack of President Yahya Khan of Pakistan and get the recognition of the world community. The world leaders to whom Maulana Bhasani sent telegrams and letters were:

1. UN Secretary General,
2. Chairman of the Peoples' Republic of China, Mao Se Tung,
3. Prime Minister of the People's Republic of China, Chou En Lai,
4. President of the Union of Soviet Socialist Republics, Nikolai Podgorny,
5. Secretary General of the Communist Party of Soviet Union, Leonid Breznev,
6. President of the United States of America, Richard M. Nixon,
7. British Prime Minister,
8. President of Yugoslavia, Marshal Josip Broz Tito,
9. President of the Republic of Egypt, Anwar el Sadaat,
10. Secretary Generals of the Arab League and the Organisation of African Unity.

'*Ganashakti*' published the opinion of all Bengal primary teachers association of the Murshidabad district branch. Alongside, it publicized the opinion of Howrah district hawkers committee's opinions. There was publicity on a large scale in the district branches of people's theatres in support of the struggle for Bangladesh. There was a request to organize working groups for popular collections. The Marxist Communist party, throughout India as also in Kolkata, was very quick to organize public opinion. The teachers and workers in Kolkata municipality and on behalf of the big tube well workers gave strong support to the ordinary people of Bangladesh, who were struggling for independence, and tried to give recognition to Bangladesh.

In another report published in '*Joi Bangla*', Pakistan President had declared that if the '*Mukti Bahini*' tried to occupy any portion of Pakistan, then they would not be alone in the declared war. Pakistan thought that when war would breakout then the United States would help Pakistan with arms and money. Pakistan also expected that once it provoked a war with India, United States's diplomatic support would be there. Perhaps the United States would come forward with food and other relief measures through the United Nations Organisation. As a result, it would be possible to put the lid over the Bangladesh situation. But ultimately Pakistan's hope ebbed away.

Thousands of doctors, nurse and medical students made protest in front of the Bangladesh deputy high commission office situated at Calcutta. They were supporting the independence movement of Bangladeshi nationals against the attack of the terrorist Yhayha Khan's rule. Sukumar Biswas points out that, on behalf of CITU, united leftist front and other democratic organizations, two processions were taken by the volunteers from tailoring shops and fan factories that penetrated many areas. They wanted to give recognition to the temporary government of independent Bangladesh, render some armaments to the '*Mukti*' forces and integrate the struggling people of Bangladesh. A medical camp was established in the India border for treatment of the ordinary people of Bangladesh, who had been affected by Pakistani military forces.

At another end, in support of the Bangladesh freedom movement, the 'Democratic Youth Federation', and Bengal Provincial students' federation organized a meeting on 10 April, at the lawn of Calcutta University that, the Trade Union Co-ordination Committee tried to organize public opinion, in order to give recognition to Bangladesh.[26] In the remote areas of West Bengal, student meetings were organized to support the freedom movement and a working committee was organized to collect money and clothing's, in order to help the people who had been badly affected. With the target of helping the freedom fighters of Bangladesh, 'Democratic Youth Federation', organized the working committees' public opinion.

Different trade union organizations in West Bengal and public organizations tried to help the people of Bangladesh, who were struggling for independence. From early April, Bangabashi College Students Union, Alipore Telegraph Store Yard, Federation club Metal Brand Engineering and other organizations gave full support to the fierce freedom fighters of Bangladesh. Different branches of the Marxist Communist Party and Students' Federation, Democratic Youth Federation, Refugee committee and others made an appeal to the local population to give support to independent Bangladesh. On 25th April, in the integration day of Bangladesh, the Marxist Communist Party of India gave a proposal to help the freedom movement of Bangladesh altogether. The Communist Party supported the struggling people of Bangladesh for the reason that: this struggle was not that of the Muslims against the Hindus, nor Biharis against the Bengalis, nor the Bengalis against the Pathans, nor that of the Bengali Muslims against the non-Bengali Muslims; it was a fight against the exploiters.

Marxist Communist Party leader Hare Krishna Kongar addressed a huge gathering on 28 May at Sonarpur, in order to help the integration of Bangladesh. He said that it was impossible to help the growth of democracy amongst the people of a foreign country, when one murders democracy in one's own country.[27]

The leaders of Indian Communist Party repeatedly uttered that, the ruling Congress destroyed democracy in India. In the pretext of giving shelter to the refugees, they gave them miserable existence. Communist Party further demanded that, Congress was much appraised in the international political arena, since it offered shelter to the refugees. Many refugees died in the meantime. Karimpur, Kalyani, Tripura and Salt Lake were places where refugee camps were established, and '*Ganashakti*' described the pathetic picture of the people in the refugee camps. The Marxist Communist Party realized at this juncture, if the Indian government helped the freedom fighters with armaments, then Bangladesh would gain independence quickly. And quicker Bangladesh would become independent, the more rapidly the refugees may return to their own country. At this moment, on the question of the recognition of Bangladesh, Congress's hesitant policy faced criticism. The reason probably was, in the first place, the dearth of direct or indirect support by the big powers, secondly the apprehension that the war would be a continuation of the previous situation between India-Pakistan, and thirdly to improve the image of the Congress in world politics by giving shelter to the refugees and in the 'Human Rights Law', was a strategy for gaining international help.

There were bitter differences among the Left groups. Some were opposed to the Liberation War, because they feared that the Bangladeshis would fall under Indian domination. Within the leftist parties, the pro-Moscow group supported the war, but the pro-Beijing factions opposed it. Many of the leftists decided to fight anyway. They said no issue takes precedence over this. They must join the liberation process.

Many former leftists became rich. Some were dacoits and crooks. Many young men and women of that time abandoned their studies to fight for the excitement of liberation. Many who joined the Left lost their livelihood, lives, everything, and were victims of the time. After more than 30 years, the Bangladeshis have still failed to achieve a national consensus. They were under military rule for 15 years. Their political institutions were not democratic, so they cannot expect democratic rule from the political parties.

Any kind of military conflict between India and Pakistan implied the strengthening of the hands of Yhayha Khan and the implications would be dangerous for the Bangladesh freedom movement.[28] '*Yhayha mereche hate, ekhane morchi bhate*', these kinds of phrases was published in '*Ganashakti*'. On the other end, Maulana Abdul Hamid Khan Bhashani's National Awami Party and like-minded other political parties, labourer and student organizations were united in a particular conference and organized 'Bangladesh nationalist freedom struggle integration committee'. The main goal of this committee was to help the progress of Bangladesh freedom struggle in a whole-hearted manner.

The relationship was already very bitter due to the situation in 1965, and the Pakistani people and the Dictator gave rise to anti-Indian sentiments. The burning sentiments of the Pakistani people were that, India was coming to the help of Pakistani people. Mrs. Indira Gandhi was touring different countries, fully aware of the situation. The Communist countries and Bhutan were getting ready to come to the help of Bangladesh.

On the question of Bangladesh, Indian Prime Minister Indira Gandhi, who was the chief of Congress, visited many countries such as, United Kingdom, United States, France, West Germany etc., in order to gain international support. On her return on 30 November Indira Gandhi declared in the Assembly, 'Pak soldiers have to be removed from Bangladesh'.[29] On 3 December, emergency was declared, when Pakistan made an air attack on India.

The promises of 1971 had been stifled before they had a chance to come to fulfillment. The teachers in Dhaka University have constructed Dhaka University cell inside the library, to preserve the history of Dhaka University. It is a valuable collection on all kinds of necessary books on Dhaka University. Another noteworthy place was Suhrawardy Uddayan, where Sheikh Mujibur Rehman used to hold public meetings. The huge park was surrounded on all sides by many trees, and at its central point was, '*Chirantan Agnisikha*' where the Pakistani army surrendered on 16 December 1971, before the Indian and East Pakistani army.

After India, recognition by Bhutan helped the democratic republic of Bangladesh to become successful. At this time, support given by different states weakened the self-confidence and bravery of Pakistani generals. The Marxist Communist Party gave the call for giving recognition to Bangladesh to different democratic countries of the world, specially the socialist countries. This was a struggle of the oppressed against the ruling community. So the U.S. capitalist powers supported the Pakistanis, although the exploited community was successful.[30]

There is much debate amongst the historians of Bangladesh on the economic and intellectual origins of the freedom movement of 1971. No definite conclusion can be drawn on the history of this freedom struggle and what kind of public opinion it raised inside and outside Bengal, Bangladesh and in the United States of America.

Notes

1. Jyoti Sengupta, *Eclipse of East Pakistan Chronicles of events since the birth of East Pakistantill October 1963*, p. 309.

2. p. 309.
3. A.F. Salahuddin Ahmed, *India Pakistan Bangladesh Perspectives on History Society Politics*, p. 42.
4. *Ibid.*, p. 92.
5. *Ibid.*, p. 92.
6. Syed Anwar Hosain, *op. cit.*, p. 145.
7. *Independence of Bangladesh in 266 Days History and Documentary Evidence*, p. 479.
8. *Ibid.*, p. 479.
9. Siddiq Salik, *Witness to surrender*, p. 105.
10. Shariyar Kabir edited, *Ekattorer Dushaho Smriti*, p. 175.
11. Sukumar Biswas, *Bangladesher Muktiyuddhe CPIM o Ganashakti*, p. 7.
12. Gita Roy, *The Duel of the Decade The U.S. Government versus the U.S. press over India's relations with Pakistan, China and Bangladesh 1962-72*, p. 125.
13. *Ibid.*, p. 126.
14. *Ibid.*, p. 127.
15. *Ibid.*, p. 127.
16. *Op. cit.*, p. 128.
17. Siddiq Salik, *Witness to Surrender*, p. 107.
18. G.W. Chowdhury, *The Last Days of East Pakistan.*
19. *Independence of Bangladesh In 266 Days History and Documentary Evidence*, Freedom Fighter Advocate Muhammad Nurul Quadir.
20. Sukumar Biswas, *Bangladesher Muktijuddhe CPIM o Ganashakti*, p. 7.
21. *Ibid.*, p. 7.
22. *Ibid.*, p. 8.
23. *Ibid.*, p. 169.
24. *Independence of Bangladesh in 266 Days: History and Documentary Evidence*, p. 79.
25. *Ibid.*, p. 78.
26. Sukumar Biswas, *Op. cit.*, p. 10.
27. *Ibid.*, p. 12.
28. Sukumar Biswas, *Bangladesher muktiyuddhe CPIM O Ganashakti*, p. 12.
29. *Ibid.*, p. 15.
30. *Ibid.*, p. 16.

7

Politics and Religion in Bangladesh 1972-75

Bordered by India on its west, north and Myanmar on the east and by the Bay of Bengal in the south, Bangladesh with over 140 million people is the most densely populated country. Having achieved its independence in December 1971, Bangladesh has been confronted with the problems of high population rate, poverty, floods and cyclones, which have been adversely affecting its economic development.

Religion: It is a small country with an area of 142,776 square kilometers only. It is geographically detached from the rest of the Muslim world. However, the overwhelming majority of population of Bangladesh are Muslims. Constitutionally also, Bangladesh is neither Islamic nor socialist. Again, politically, Bangladesh is a playground for all. There are pro-India, pro-Russia, pro-America and pro-China political parties in Bangladesh. And, Jamaat-e-Islami was at the vanguard of the Islamic movement in Bangladesh. Jamaat-e-Islami Bangladesh upholds Islam in its entirety. It aims at bringing about changes in all phases and spheres of human activities on the basis of the guidance revealed by Allah and exemplified by his Prophet Mohammed. Thus the Jamaat-e-Islami Bangladesh is at the same time a religious, political, social and cultural movement.

Sharing a common land border of over 4,100 kms, both Bangladesh and India are bound by age old traditions, culture and history. Therefore, illegal immigration of over 15 million Bangladeshi nationals to India has changed the demographic profile of some north-eastern states of

India, besides increasing pressure on land and resources causing social tension. Bangladesh's failure to cooperate with India in the repatriation of illegal Bangladeshi immigrants has complicated the problem. After liberation of 1971, their representatives asked for autonomy for the Chakmas and other *Adivasis*, with their own representatives.

From 1971, various changes have occurred in the socio-economic and political fields. The country has experienced various political regimes. The changing nature of political economy shaped the nature of dominance and its policies. The tenure of Sheikh Mujibur Rahman was marked by civilian supremacy in the political arena.

Bangladesh became independent under the leadership of *Awami* League with its leader Sheikh Mujibur Rehman. Though Bangladesh started with fragile political and economic systems, but within a short span of time, *Awami* League government was able to establish its authority and build political and economic institutions.

According to historian A.F. Salahuddin Ahmed, basically, the Awami League was a constitutional political party.[1] Its leadership was acquainted with the mechanism and practices of constitutional politics. It was impossible on its part to undertake a well-planned revolutionary programme of action or evolve a strategy to meet a crisis.

Constitution: The state formulated a new constitution within nine months of independence and national election in 1973. The government established different national political institutions including cabinet, parliament, judiciary, election and planning commission. The first government of this new state of Bangladesh was made up of an apparent dichotomy. On the one hand, Bangladesh was the second largest Muslim state in the world after Indonesia. On the other hand and paradoxically for many Muslims, it proclaimed a secular polity. This is a unique phenomenon.

Independent Bangladesh emerged in December 1971, as a small nation in south Asia, on the strength of Bengali nationalism and as a secular country. However, after the assassination of Sheikh Mujib-ur-Rahman in 1975, Bengali nationalism of the pre and post-liberation period was replaced by Bangladeshi nationalism. Now, the secular principle of the constitution of 1972 was dropped and the Islamic orientation of the polity became pronounced.

The political-bureaucratic-military elite started using Islam to legitimize their leadership. Bangladesh now sought to emphasise its links with the Islamic *Ummah* and stressed to maintain special relations with the Islamic countries. This shift in its foreign policy brought Bangladesh certain economic benefits in terms of liberal assistance by the West Asian countries and consequent easing of pressure on its oil import bill. The country witnessed the resurgence of Islamic fundamentalism, as *Jamaat-e-Islami* and other Islamic outfits such as *Islamic Chatro Shibir* and *Islami Oikyo Jote* consolidated and expanded their institutional network fully utilizing Islamic petro dollars. Of late, the existence of Islamist militant underground groups such as *Harkat-ul-Jihad-e-Islami* (HUJI), *Hizbul Mujahideen*, *Lashkar-e-Taiba*, *Jaish-e-Mohammed* in Bangladesh and their continued anti-India activities, has been a major security threat to India.

The aims and objects of the Jamaat-e-Islami Bangladesh: These urge upon all human beings in general and the Muslims in particular to respond to the following calls:

(i) Accept Allah, the Lord of the Universe as the only sovereign and his last Prophet Mohammed, peace be upon him

(ii) Make objective efforts to establish the law of Allah and the rule of the pious with a view to eradicating all forms of oppression and exploitation aiming at providing full justice to people at large.

The Jamaat-e-Islami Bangladesh aims at bringing about a revolution. In their opinion, if Allah, the Lord of the universe, grants opportunity, the Jamaat-e-Islami Bangladesh, backed by people's support, may form government and mould the whole society and the state in accordance with the dictates of the Quran and the Sunnah. With this end in view, the Jamaat-e-Islami has chalked out a four-point programme:

(i) *Tabligh* and *Dawah* (Propagation and Call),

(ii) *Tanzeem* and *Tarbiah* (Organisation and Training),

(iii) *Islah al-Ijtimayee* (Social Reforms) and

(iv) *Islah al Hukumah* (to reform the government and administration).

There were street-posters saying, 'Accept Gaulam Azam as a citizen of Bangladesh.' However, he was hated, because the Jama'at e-Islami had been against the freedom of Bangladesh. Gaulam Azam had gone to Pakistan at the time of independence. A small item appeared in the papers, saying he had returned to Bangladesh because his mother was ill.

Contemporary booklets written by Golam Azam points out that, the politicians of West Pakistan were not satisfied with the freedom that has been given by Sheikh Mujibur Rehman. They did not believe in the independence of Bangladesh. The clandestine forces present within Bangladesh tried to sabotage and demolish the newly-founded state, based on linguistic nationalism. In one pamphlet, for instance, '*Mediar Mukhomukhi Golam Azam* ', the former *Ameer* of *Jamat* gave his opinion that the freedom won with the help of Indian Prime Minister Indira Gandhi, was not covetable. Secular and democratic politics was not getting the upper hand.

Jeremy Seabrook describes that, in a modest monsoon-stained building close to a congested railway crossing in Moghbazar is an office of the Jama'at-e-Islami[2] : a frugal interior, dingy curtains at the doors, metal grilles at the windows, gunmetal *almirahs* (cupboards), where he met Abul Qader Mullah. He was a senior party member, who studied Physics and later became a teacher. Originally within the leftist movement, he turned his attention to how Islamic morality might be introduced into Leftist ideology. This led him to study Islam in greater depth, and as a result, he embraced Islam totally.

Any sane and adult person can become a member of the Jamaat-e-Islami Bangladesh if he or she accepts the basic creed of the Jamaat-e-Islami as his or her own aims and objects, pledges to fulfill the demands of the constitution of the Jamaat-e-Islami, performs the obligatory duties ordained by Islam, refrains from major sins, adopting any means of livelihood forbidden by Islam and does not encroach upon the rights of others and does not associate himself or herself with any other parties or association, the creed, aims and objects and principles of which clash with those of Jamaat-e-Islami Bangladesh.

There were indications that certain ultra-conservative religious parties, notably the fundamentalist *Jamaat-e-Islami*, were forming working relations with certain left-wing organizations, who had their own reasons for opposing Mujib. The rapidly growing popularity of Maulana Bhasani, who had managed to combine a respect for traditional Islam with a vaguely defined pro-Chinese socialism, was an indicator of such trend in politics. In Mujib's time, there was a strong tilt towards Islam because Mujib had to make room for the petro-dollar rich Gulf States and Saudi Arabia (due to the extreme financial difficulties of new-born state). Certain policy adjustments were made in domestic affairs also, thus giving Islam a prominent role than before. The Islamic foundation, which had been abolished after independence, revived by a presidential proclamation in March 1975 and Mujib himself began attending Islamic gatherings in a routine manner. Bangladesh needed financial assistance and during the initial years in 1973-4, it received about $200 million Saudi aid, this went up to 1 billion dollar in 1978. During the Second Five Year Plan period (1980-5) this aid was much higher. The participants in the aid programme to Bangladesh included other oil-rich countries in the region.

Bangladesh was also dependent on the Middle East for the supply of her total need of crude oil. During 1974-5, Iran and Abu Dhabi, in particular, were approached by Bangladesh for supply of crude oil on a long-term basis. Annual import bill with regard to crude oil alone stood at taka 200 crore in 1974-5. In 1975, Bangladesh was required to pay about taka 200 crore in excess of this amount, for oil imports as a result of the decision of the OPEC, in favour of a 10 per cent rise in oil prices. During the same period almost two-third of Bangladesh's foreign exchange earnings were spent on import of oil estimated at 14 lakh tones per annum. The help coming from Arab countries made them look like Islamic benefactors of Bangladesh. Bangladesh was certainly coming close to Islamic brotherhood on economic grounds and this had its impact on Bangladesh, pulling her towards fundamentalism.

A thorough study of the *Quran* and the *Hadith* would point out that, the right to property and such other humanitarian notions have been interpreted many times. So far as the women's question is concerned, it is a known fact that the *Quran* gave many rights to women and spelt them out in detail and the relevant verses which may be reinterpreted as something that implies freedom and dignity for women. While the *Quran* treats women with dignity and accords them equal status with men in most ways, Muslim tradition, practices and customary law (*Shariyat*) has deviated from it and is often found to be highly prejudicial to women, treating them as far more inferior to men. The tradition, "that nation can never prosper which has assigned its reign to a woman", has been taken very seriously in many cases in Islamic countries. The women of Bangladesh as they are projected in the society should be analysed in the context of true and honest Quranic laws. In Bangladesh specifically, the right to property has changed, with the transformation from democracy to dictatorship many times, and the 'Enemy Properties Act', renamed as, 'Vested Properties Act' (1974) has been studied. There has been large-scale migration from Bangladesh to India, along with the exchange of landed property. It can hardly be said that the Quranic verses are extended and accepted.

The civil society of Bangladesh fought the state of Pakistan resolutely during 1947-71 in order to replace theocracy by democracy, and following the long struggle since 1947-8, the foundations of a strong civil society was laid during 1971-5. Some new administrative arrangements were to come into effect in September 1975, but on 15 August, Bangabandhu Sheikh Mujibur Rehman and many of his family members were cruelly assassinated. The basic character of the constitution of 1972 was disfigured by anti-secular forces after the assassination of Sheikh Mujib. With General Ziaur Rehman as the Army Chief and Justice A.M. Sayem as the President of the country, politics in Bangladesh acquired similar characteristics to that of Pakistan politics during 1958-68.

In was an interview of Golam Azam taken by BBC, Golam Azam was asked about the reason why he refrained himself from participating in the '*Muktijuddha*' of 1971.[3] He replied that the war of 1971 had been thrust upon the Bangladeshis by India, and most of the Islamic parties did not participate in this war.

Muktijuddha was a work done by Zulfiqar Ali Bhutto and others, and even Sheikh Mujibur Rehman did not want such independence. A number of pamphlets were purchased by his party, '*Jamaat-e-Islami*', on the concept of Allah, Islamic and Shariyat laws. These were written by other members of '*Jamaat-e-Islami*', such as Khandakar Abdul Khayer or Abbas Ali Khan.

At the opposite pole is the '*Ekattorer Ghatak Dalal Nirmul Committee*' that publicized posters demanding the exclusion of Golam Azam and his effigy burning at the public place called 'Suhrawardy Uddayan'. The writings, essays and articles by the leftist writers who deal with Bangladesh nationalism, show significant research. One of the chief proponents of this movement is Shariyar Kabir, who has edited many books, such as, *Ekattorer Dushaho Smriti*, where he has elaborated on different levels of torture on the victims of 1971. There have been relics of '*ganakabar*' or mass burial in Chattagram and other areas. The example of genocide on Bangladesh by the West Pakistani army gathered much criticism in world public opinion. Different newspapers in the foreign countries, starting from '*Anandabazar Patrika*' and '*Ganashakti*' in India, up to the correspondents of New York Times in America, give a vivid description of one of the worst genocides in the world, carried out by the Islamic fundamentalists. After democracy returned to Bangladesh, Sukumar Biswas, Syed Anwar Hosain and other activists tried to construct 'oral history' of Bangladesh freedom movement, to encounter the voices of those victims who have been totally lost. But there are many hindrances in this process, as the victims of rape, sexual abuse and other kinds of inhuman torture were mostly reluctant to open their mouth and talk freely. On the side of the rightists, the Ramkrishna Mission *Sannyasis* in Dhaka are not too eager to speak about the destructive forces that had dealt a blow on their '*math*' many times.

When we went to Bangladesh for a field-trip in May 2001, the so-called '*Maharaja's* extended their hospitality to us, and it was an atmosphere of cultural heritage inside the mission. The '*Dhaka Kalibari*', a very old institution, was destroyed many times and had to be rebuilt again. There are very few victims who would write down the elaboration of the massacare, how the Pakistani army made tortures by piercing needles inside the body or they were annihilated by iron rods.[4]

Economy: After liberation, marginal farmers who did not have landholding rights but had a kind of possess ional right, lost their land through debt, poverty, and dowry or by being cheated. With the disruption of war and the return of refugees, the personnel of the Land Settlement Office were susceptible to bribes and corruption. In the year 1976, a group of young people called the landless together in a collective effort to recover lands, records of which had been falsified by the privileged rich who had taken possession of them. The ratio of landless increased in Bangladesh from 31 per cent of the population in 1971 to about 67 per cent in 2001. Most *khas* land—had been occupied by 'landlords'. Eighty per cent of the people of Bangladesh worked in agriculture, but they own only 5 per cent of the country's resources. Even after independence, this was the condition.

According to findings, even during Mujib's time, the economy was not really strong at the basis. The main crop production of the country was jute, and writers Atiur Rehman and Lenin Azad in a series on the language movement, showed how this industry was bifurcated and suffered a lot, after 1947. Before 1971, the military dictators tried to reap all the profit that was gained from this industry and the Mujib government could not make much headway about it.

BRAC, a national private development organization, set up in 1972 by Fazle Hasan Abed was initially established as a relief organisation, to afford assistance to resettle refugees floating from India after the liberation war. The immediate task of rehabilitation over, BRAC turned to focus on the long-term use of poverty alleviation and empowerment of the poor, especially women, in the rural areas of Bangladesh.

From its modest beginning in 1972 BRAC, Bangladesh Rural Advancement Committee is a multi-faceted organization with over 26,000 regular staff and 36,000 part-time teachers, working in 60, 627 villages in all the 64 districts of Bangladesh.[5] BRAC has been characterized as a learning institution, from experience and through a responsive and inductive process. The task of BRAC is to diagnose poverty in real human terms. Mahbubul Karim, senior vice-president of Proshika, joined BRAC soon after the war of 1971.

Jeremy Seabrook's companion in Bangladesh was Abdur Rob, who ran the Cultural Development Programme of Proshika, and whose story itself exemplified the psychological and social journey through disillusion, and the hope of renewal. After the war, he wanted Bangladesh to be the happiest country in the world, with democracy and plenty. They fought for emancipation of the people, and they thought this would then happen. By 1972-3, they saw many in the Awami League grow rich, even some who had fought with them.

As to the question of agricultural production, it has to be ascertained whether the women in different villages worked as agricultural labourers, and when they migrate across the border to India, they often work as seasonal or temporay wage-labourers. They hardly had any passport or ration-card, and they often migrate from the porous borders of Bangladesh into the foothills of northern Bengal region, and help in the production of food crops. What kind of wages they earn from the plantations, whether they abide by the rules laid down in the different regulations by the government, is a matter of controversy and requires much survey and fieldwork. The female and child labourers are the worst sufferers in this matter, since they often give the maximum hours of labour and they are deprived of their regular wages. They are often below the poverty-line, poor and undernourished. This is a problem that has been faced since colonial times. Hill women in the Chittagong Hill Tracts are frank, humourous and visible in contrast to their Bengali counterparts. They enormously contribute to the building of their families and communities. But they are defenseless against human rights abuses including rape. It may be noted that Bangladesh state has continuously rejected the notion of giving indigenous status to the hill people, since according to international law that meant conceding them certain land rights. Therefore, the women of the Chittagong Hill Tracts have been negotiating conflict both in the public and private spheres.

The education of the minority community of women in Bangladesh, such as the Buddhists and tribal people in the Chittagong Hill Tracts and the declining Hindu community, their problems and demands, have to be taken into consideration and their literature and opinion have to be looked into. Bangladesh went through a series of changes, alternatively with democracy and dictatorship, and the challenges undertaken in the educational policy, and the significance of '*madrasah*' education has to be comprehended.

Freedom unfinished Fundamentalism and popular resistance in Bangladesh Today, written by Jeremy Seabrook, describes a journey through Bangladesh between 1999 and 2000; through the seasons and landscapes, the social and moral sensibility, the cultural and political struggles of the country. Here Seabrook describes that the villages of Bangladesh are beautiful—houses of clay or tin, the shade of spreading trees, beaten mud floors, fragrant fodder and grasses, courtyards with hens and ducks. The towns were the symbols of the collapse of ancient agrarian culture, the destination of the defeated; towns gave grudging shelter to an injured, wasting peasantry; they represented loss of land, therefore of meaning and according to Seabrook, the poorest part of Bangladesh was a small town near Dinajpur. So *Proshika* grew out of the disillusionment of the mid-1970s.

Its stand against fundamentalism, social injustice, elites, and in favour of minorities—Hindu, Christian and indigenous peoples—and specially in favour of the participation of women in the economy and society, brought it into sometimes violent conflict with other social forces, both within and outside Bangladesh.

The Bangladeshi nationalists of the Bangladesh National Party were intolerant of the hill people, because they are Buddhists. Jeremy Seabrook's purpose is to show, as clearly possible, the struggle between the older, humanistic Bengali tradition-secular, with the concept of a narrower, conservative Bangladeshi nationalism, underpinned by the disciplines of a redefined, fundamentalist Islam.

After liberation, religious-based political parties were outlawed. They were basically communal parties two main parties that deny each other's right to rule. The distant reason for this may be found in the bitter but inconclusive struggles between Bangladeshi identity and Bengali identity. The role of India in supplying support and refuge to Bangladeshi freedom fighters in 1971 was an irksome reminder of its power.

The liberation war and the creation of Bangladesh in 1971 appeared to resolve the issue. Sheikh Mujibur Rahman was undisputed leader, and his Awami League came to power with overwhelming popular support. The dreams of the liberation of Bangladesh from its status as East Pakistan were soon destroyed by the miserable reality of destitution and impoverishment which it inherited after the *muktijudda*, the war of independence. It says much of the psyche of Bengal that people truly expected to enter into the patrimony of *sonar Bangla*—the golden Bengal of its poetry and literature, a mythic place of freedom and plenty—soon as foreign domination was ended. Such was their faith; it seems the Bangladeshis believed in the power of imagination to transform their shattered, beautiful land. When the military took over less than five years after Independence, overt political activity was impossible.

The journey out of Dhaka passed through choking fogs of dusty pollution over the almost stationary traffic. A degraded, semi-industrialised countryside marked the gravitational pull of the capital, which was itself like the intensifying core of a cyclone, sucking resources to its center, uprooting villages, excavating paddy-fields.

The road towards the crossing at Aricha was a thread of small settlements, no longer villages, not quite towns. In their markets, plastic goods have displaced older bamboo artifacts, just as tin has replaced the houses' bamboo and reed roofs, an urbanizing limbo which parallels the industrializing of agriculture. The tin is new; corrugated roofs gleam in the sunlight. Tin is not cheaper than clay or bamboo, but it lasts longer, and is secure against rain or wind, not against cyclones, however, which scatter tin and turn it into a dangerous projectile.

The ferry is a huge rusting structure. A man of about 50, unsmiling, bitter, he was a freedom fighter in 1971. After the war, he was rewarded with a job as a truck-driver with the Special Branch. After the assassination of Sheikh Mujib, he was dismissed, since the military replaced all government personnel. He was a truck driver, taking bricks to Dhaka. He says many freedom fighters were disabled; they still lack land and live in want.

The choice is not between Bengali culture and Islamic culture: the demands of religion have always co-existed with the Bengali sensibility, although the asperities of fundamentalism cannot. That this drama should be unfolding in a wider context of globalisation and in the shadow of an India increasingly under the sway of Hindu fundamentalism only adds further dimensions of uncertainty and confusion to the still unresolved struggle. Actually, there is hardly any clash between Islamic religion and Bengali culture. Unfortunately, however, the former was trying to swallow up the latter.

The relief and rehabilitation after the war brought a good deal of foreign help to the country, and many idealistic young Bangladeshis were drawn to make a contribution to their stricken land; this impulse was given a further push by dawning realization that the values for which they thought that the war had been fought were in danger of being lost.

It is true that Sheikh Mujib's government had its limitations and failings. The government might have committed many mistakes. But it must be remembered that the Bangabandhu's government was a popular government, duly elected by the sovereign people of Bangladesh. The people alone had the right to change the government, could have been brought about either through constitutional means or by revolutionary popular upheaval. But nothing of that sort happened on 15 August 1975, when Sheikh Mujib was brutally killed by a gang of armymen, and the military takeover of the state and the intrusion of armed men in the political arena continues to pose a serious threat to democracy in Bangladesh.[6]

The country failed to produce a true democracy. Then from 1975 military dictatorship lasted till 1991. So in May 1975, the military trial of 36 air force people began. Even before 1975, Maulana Bhasani had set up the *Shantibahini*. So, when Sheikh Mujib was murdered in a coup in 1975, the exhausted country did not respond with a display of anger. When the military took over less than five years after Independence, overt political activity was impossible.

The question arises, why Sheikh Mujib was assassinated. Everything seemed to be normal. They did not realize the basic factors. It is a grim fact that, 'the Father of the nation' was murdered in this way and a few observations may be made about it. The politics of this era proves that, the basis of the nation that Sheikh Mujib had built up was not really strong enough; they drifted towards easily the murder of a person who had given them freedom. A comparable case-study may be that of the assassination of Mohandas Karamchand Gandhi at Noakhali on the eve of India's partition, who was a preacher of non-violence but his life was brought to an end abruptly by Nathuram Godsey.

Notes

1. A.F. Salahuddin Ahmed, *India Pakistan Bangladesh Perspectives on History Society and Politics*, p. 92.
2. Jeremy Seabrook, *Fundamentalism.*
3. *Mediar Mukhomukhi Golam Azam.*
4. Shariyar Kabir edited *Ekattorer Dushaho Smriti*, p. 11.
5. Jeremy Seabrook, *Freedom Unfinished.*
6. A.F. Salahuddin Ahmed, *India Pakistan Bangladesh Perspectives on History Society and Politics*, p. 93.

8

Religious Currents and Cross-Currents 1975-90

Sukumar Biswas and Hiroshi Sato studied how religion acted frequently as the main factor in a community which did not yet formulate or was unable to create a platform for total national awakening.[1] Their joint work was an outcome of the collaboration of two separate studies, one on the period before the liberation of Bangladesh, and the other after it.[2] The second part of the study analyses the political backdrop of the much-debated policy of Islamization in the post-liberation phase of Bangladesh.[3]

According to Hiroshi Sato, an apparent lack of ideological coherence in the 'Islamisation' of Bangladesh was very prominent in comparison with the same process observed in Pakistan, where an official body of the Council of Islamic ideology had formulated the policies to be observed by the secular administration.[4] Furthermore, in East Pakistan, the strong nationalist tradition, which got as far back as the language movement in the 1950s, and autonomy war right upto 1971 when the country was liberated after a bloody struggle, has stood in the way of an unfettered 'Islamisation' of the state.

The Mujib government was replaced in 1975 by an army who staged a coupd'etat, killed most of his family members and other senior party leaders, and seized control of the government. Since then, Bangladesh had passed through fitful political changes; and government in power lacked popular support and stability. Islam proved handy to such rulers in appealing to the sentiments of the people and assured them of a certain degree of legitimacy. Though Sheikh Mujib had himself depended on Islam as a factor that could make its influence felt on various aspects of state-administration, it was given speed and dynamism by the subsequent military-bureaucratic regimes of Ziaur Rehman and Hosain Mohammed Ershad in the 1980s.

The dependence on the Middle Eastern countries for a vital supply (oil) produced a number of results favouring the rise of Islamic symbols in national life. There was a steady growth of what may be termed as Institutional Islam, backed by a huge injection of petro-dollars.[5] Also, there was a growing tendency in the past two decades to display Arabic bill-boards at public places, posting of citations from the 'Quran' on office walls and private and public transports and buildings, use of the media, radio and television, in particular, to propagate Islamic materials, and the beautification of mosques.[6] These steps had often been taken to please the visiting Arab dignitaries and create an Islamic sentiment among the ordinary people.

One of the major aims of Bangladesh was to win over moral and diplomatic support from Islamic countries. It was necessary to consolidate her position in the comity of nations. The attempts brought good results because it was found that she was gradually admitted as a member of the Organisation of Islamic countries. This aim was largely fulfilled since she received support from her brother countries at the time of being a member of the World Health Organisation and the United Nations. A country which was born out of a fight for linguistic nationalism was tilting on religiosity for the development of a community and nation.

Syed Anwar Hossain points out that, "Courting of diplomatic favours of the Muslim Middle East remains a major goal of Bangladesh foreign policy".[7] Hence she constantly endeavours to show her willingness to work as a full-fledged member of the Islamic Ummah and there is a growing Islamic orientation of the ruling elite in Bangladesh with frequent references to Islam as the desired basis of state ideology.

To Pakistan, as also to the pro-Pakistani forces in Bangladesh-secularism was untouchable. Thus, within a few hours following the assassination of Sheikh Mujib, Radio Pakistan announced that Bangladesh banished secularism by the establishment of an independent Republic. As early as December 1975, when Justice A.M. Sayem was the country's President, and General Zia was the defacto power behind him, a martial law proclamation repealed a sub-clause of Article 66 and Article 122 of the constitution of 1972, thus removed the legal provisions which prevented the opponents of the 1971 freedom struggle from giving them in the voters' rights in the Bangladesh *Jatiye Sangsad*. This was definitely a blow for the liberal-minded section of the people of Bangladesh. A large majority of these persons, opposed to the independence of Bangladesh, were members of Islamic parties and Article 38 of the 1972 Constitution had imposed a ban upon political parties on religion, but, a martial law proclamation of 1976 removed this procedure. It paved the way to the resurgence of pro-Pakistan Islamic parties in Bangladesh. Zia at heart never believed in the resurgence of Bengalees as a nation, and the country by and large. He introduced Bangladeshi nationalism in place of Bengali which was secular in essence. Zia amply demonstrated his loyalty to Pakistan when he took steps to win the referendum in May 1977 and consolidate his autocracy. The replacement of Bengali nationalism by Bangladeshi nationalism was another step in moulding an anti-secular state and in order to demonstrate the Islamic orientation of the constitution, the martial law proclamation of April 1977 inserted the following words on the top of the Preamble to the constitution: 'In the name of Allah, the Beneficent, the Merciful'. After the abandonment of the law that made the political parties based on religion illegal, the fundamentalist politics in Bangladesh received new impetus and the fundamentalists started organizing themselves in different political parties.

In five years General Ziaur Rehman amended the constitution of Bangladesh in order to espouse the doctrine of Bangladeshi nationalism. Khondkar Abdul Hamid known for his loyalty to Pakistan was the exponent of this doctrine. In February 1976, in the course of a speech in the Bangla Academy at Dhaka, Hamid said that it was appropriate to characterize the nationalism of his countrymen as Bangladeshi patriotism. This nationalism represented a glorious identity born of history, tradition, art, literature, sculpture and a unique philosophy of life, collective psychology and aspirations. All these traits separated Bangladeshis from all other Muslim entities of the world—even from the Bengali speaking Muslims in other countries and regions. Hamid explained that he talked of Islam as a culture because 85 per cent of the Bangladeshis were Muslims. Hamid concluded that the above noted elements underlined by him formed the essence, foundation and strength of Bangladeshi nationalism. Religion was an essential component of this concept of Bangladeshi nationalism, whereas Bengali nationalism accepted secularism as one of its foundations. This became quite evident when at the biennial council session of the Awami League (1981), General Secretary Abdur Razzaq accused Zia of distorting the meaning of Bengali nationalism nourished through a hundred years because Zia replaced democracy by autocracy and eliminated secularism to spread communalism.

The police fired upon Rajshahi University students on 20 March 1978 and there was a procession in Dhaka protesting against police atrocities in Rajshahi. The Dhaka police too opened fire and at that time four student organizations—the Bangladesh Chhatra League, Bangladesh Chhatra Union, Bangladesh Chhatra Samiti and Bangladesh *Biplabi Chhatra* Union—came together to form a Kendriya Sangram Parishad. At Bangladesh Agricultural University too, similar incidents took place, and three students died.

The situation was very complex, dangerous, provoking and bad. At the time of partition, in 1947, there was a significant exodus of Hindus, which was repeated after 1971. The problem of Islamization had its impact on society and culture. Bengali culture—pluralist, humanist, rooted with its songs, dance, folklore, drama and literature—confronted the austere discipline of Islam in Bangladesh. The confusion this creates is immobilization of the society, and helps to explain the stagnation of Bangladesh, the slow pace of development, the survival of feudal dues, and the persistence of poverty. Azhar says, he is 'first Bengali, then Muslim.' This version of identity is particularly significant in Bangladesh and now becoming rare. Bengali identity precedes Bangladeshi identity.

Much funding for resistance to fundamentalism came from the west. According to Jeremy Seabrook and many other writers, several organizations such as the United Nations and other Human Rights institutions always tried to maintain peace in South Asia. This predisposed the recipients to leniency towards western dominance, and a group within Bangladesh became more westernized than others, as Western capital flowed into Bangladesh industry through several channels.

The crucial difference is between religion and fundamentalism. The fundamentalists sponsor 'Borkha's and they are anti-modernization and anti-equality between men and women in the field of education. They do not give equal status to Muslim women. They detest merriment such as songs and dances. The fundamentalists always detest men and women singing and performing together. The fundamentalists always try to help and convert the poor and the best measure for judging poverty in rural Bangladesh is the number of months of sufficiency and scarcity.

Golam Azam represented the pro-Pakistanis and the leader of Jamaat and declared in an interview with the BBC that only Indian supremacy would be established when East Pakistan gained independence. He is described as the projection of manpower in this area and is a shown as a relative of lakhs of people in this area. His projected political life extended for more than fifty years. Starting with the language movement till the movements against military administration, Golam Azam played a prominent role in the political affairs of the country. He was connected with Ja'mat politics for long forty-five years. Within this time, he became the Secretary of Ja'mat in contemporary East Pakistan for thirteen years, and then became the provincial *Amir* in the year 1969. From '72 to '78, he was obliged to lead a refugee life at London because of his opposition and defiance to the liberation movement. However, after Mujib's demise, and during Zia-ur-Rehman's administration, he was allowed to return to the country. After returning to the country in '78, Golam Azam was elected the *Amir* of Ja'mat-e-Islami. Till 2000, he held a responsible position as *Amir* of Ja'mat. He was elected the *Amir* after three year gaps. The popularity of Golam Ajam was made focused by the newspapers. The paper, '*Dainik Shangram*' took an intensive interview of Golam Azam. In this intimate interview, Golam Ajam described the different events of his long, colourful, political life, his childhood and student life, his proud role in the language movement, description of different events and political leaders, movements in politics and different questions regarding Bangladesh's future and distinct events of Jamat-e-Islami. Taking the advantage of extreme poverty of the people of Bangladesh, the *Jamaati*s organized their workers. Golam Azam had come to Bangladesh several times with a Pakistani passport during the rule of Zia and Ershad, but his appeal for citizenship was refused by the home ministry since he was one of the main war criminals of 1971. In his views, Islamization is the last thing in the world. He had a deep faith in Islam with all its militant aspects. Whatever is happening, Islam is democratic, a religion of well-being of the people. It is a Hegelian concept, where the Creator and the Created—they are the same. He projects Islam as the saviours of humanity. In a conversation with Golam Azam, I had a clear idea of his views, regarding the role of Islam as a useful and benevolent element for humanity.

In August 1977, the government of Bangladesh took the initiative of forming a commission for writing the history of the liberation war under the name, *Bangladesh Swadhinata Juddha Itihash Prakalpo*, to be headed by the famous poet Hasan Hafizur Rehman. A fifteen volume collection of documents edited by Hassan Hafizur Rehman, and published by the government of Bangladesh (Dhaka 1982-85), that begins with the proclamation announcing the partition of Bengal in 1905. It does not state why it begins with the first partition, as it does not and possibly cannot produce any document as evidence of some public activity, demanding a separate Bengal for the Bengali Muslims. Thus the *BSJD* (Volume 1) opens with the government order of 1905 and then makes a jump to 1940, i.e., the year of the Lahore Resolution. It gives a vivid description of the different parliamentary debates in the constituent Assembly of East Pakistan after 1947.

The Commission undertook the task of collecting various documents around the world and particularly inside the country, pertaining to the liberation war and appointed an experts committee for authentication and credential work. The committee included eminent historians and academics like Salahuddin Ahmed, Anisuzzaman, Emanul Haque, K.M. Mohsin and other prominent names. Work started in 1978 January and within 1985 June, 15 volumes of documents were published under the title, *Bangladesher Swadhinata Juddha Dalilpatra*. Each volume contains an editorial introduction. The editor declared that it was difficult to avoid subjectivity in the historical writings on a momentous event like 1971 and therefore the primary task had been set towards the collection and publication of documents.

Ranabir Samaddar explains that some of these documents have brought out the revolutionary activities led by Siraj Sikdar '*Purba Bangla Sarbahara Party* ', where they tried to pursue the tactics of united national front on an independent basis.[8] Samaddar further points out that, here in this history is a case of double irony: the more one sinks into the world of archives to realize an authentic, comprehensive "history" of 1971, there are much differences.[9] Yet these differences compel Ranabir Smaddar and the writers of BSJD to produce a totality which cannot be different from the scripts (the "*kathika*"s) of the Radio Bangladesh in Mujibngar, 1971.

The desperate endeavour to impose a totality in 1971 is very clear from this document. At the same time the document makes clear how this totality is ridden with differential traces. Indeed the same archival source has a document titled, Bangladesh *Jatiyo Mukti Sangram Samannoy Committeer Ghoshona*, (The Declaration of the Bangladesh National Liberation Struggle Committee) 1st June, 1971. This document speaks of the actors whom the history of 1971 has not endowed with the best of glory, like Maulana Bhasani, Diben Sikdar led Purba Bangla Communist Party and many others.

It is noteworthy that, the majority in Bangladesh are uneducated and poor. Their superstition has been capitalized and they have a limited view on religion, so '*Fatwa*'s have been circulated one after another. Not that there has not been much resistance against this, but the protest raised by the ordinary people have not received much support—due to the failure of the educated community and the imbalance of the politicians.

A thorough study of the *Quran* and the *Hadith* would show that, the right to property and such humanitarian notions have been interpreted many times. So far as the women's question is concerned, the *Quran* gives many rights to women and spelt them out in details. The relevant verses of the *Quran* may be interpreted in favour of dignity and freedom for women. While the *Quran* treats women with dignity and accords them equal status with men in most ways, Muslim tradition, practices and customary law (*Shariat*) has deviated from it and is often found to be highly prejudicial to women, treating them as far more inferior to men. The tradition, "that nation can never prosper which has assigned its reign to a woman", has been taken very seriously in many cases in Islamic countries. The women of Bangladesh as they are projected in society should be analysed in the context of true and honest Quranic laws. In Bangladesh specifically, the right to property has changed, with the transformation from democracy to dictatorship many times, and the 'Enemy Properties Act' renamed as, 'Vested Properties Act' (1974) has been studied. There has been large-scale migration from Bangladesh to India, along with the exchange of landed property. It can hardly be said that the Quranic verses are extended and accepted.

The anti-liberation forces were stronger now than they had been at any time since the war. Anti-Indian sentiment is also there. The Muslims would make an alliance with the most fervid fundamentalists because of their loathing of Hindus. The Nazis in Germany said what the fundamentalists were saying now, both in India and Bangladesh, and indeed in Pakistan also: just as Hitler said Aryans were the master race, Muslims say that only Islam holds truth, as according to the theory of Golam Azam.

NGOs were raising their heads, they were anti-fundamentalist. A few words may be said about the NGOs which came at that time. In the early days, NGOs were criticized from left and right. Rightists said they were agents of Communism, and Leftists said they were imperialists. The Right also said that it was the mission of NGOs to make people Christian. This came from those NGOs now called fundamentalists, but at the time they were just seen as religious groups.[10] *Proshika*, one such NGO, worked for the economic and political emancipation of the poor, the equality and liberation of women, human rights and democratic perception; and against fundamentalism, exclusivist, communalism, privilege and the defence of feudalism.

Bodhan, the leading group of *Proshika*'s cultural network, is dedicated to conserving and enhancing Bengali culture. It ran a school, teaching drama, folk-themes, dance, dialogue, story-telling, ballad-singing, recitation, choral work and song; a rich storehouse of tradition; but more significantly, a resource in the struggle against fundamentalism.

Zia was assassinated in 1981, and a subsequent coup in 1982 brought General Ershad to power. Military rule remained until 1991. That year saw the election of Khaleda Zia, widow of Zia ur-Rahman and inheritor of his Bangladesh National Party. She, in turn, was defeated in 1996 by Sheikh Hasina, daughter of Sheikh Mujib and leader of the Awami League. Therefore, personal enmity between the two women has helped to freeze the politics of Bangladesh.

Hossain Mohammed Ershad was the head of a military dominated government marked by denationalization and privatization in the economic arena. Begum Khaleda Zia headed a civilian dominated government and propagated economic liberalism, while Sheikh

Hasina Wajed had similar government as of economic liberalism. Each government had distinct characters in political, power structure and policy aspects.

Valley of Humiliation: On 30 May 1981, General Ziaur Rehman was murdered by a few officers of the army in the seaport Chattagram, 200 miles from the capital Dhaka. Following Zia's assassination, Ershad ruled Bangladesh for about nine years from 1982 to 1990. General Husain Mohammed Ershad, like his predecessor Ziaur Rehman, was keen on establishing conservative Islamic traditions and keep away from democracy. He began early to interfere in civil administration and he definitely took a dip in fundamentalism to consolidate his power and influence. In his time, the fundamentalist tenets came back within a constitutional outfit. His device to moot Islamic traditions in Bangladesh was by means of constitutional amendments.

On 15 January 1985, General Ershad dismissed his Council of Ministers and abolished special martial courts to give Bangladesh a religious structure through constitutional measures. The Eighth Amendment to the Constitution (7 June 1986) was the most harmful attack by Ershad on the civil society and it declared Islam as the state religion. Shekh Hasina announced that the declaration of Islam as a state-religion was a treachery against the three million martyrs of the struggle for independence. At the constitutional level, Islam was considered an essential element of national identity. Declaring Islam as a state religion instead of announcing Bangladesh to be an Islamic republic was (unlike Zia) a cautious approach. This would look like nothing but a constitutional amendment and the deep-set implications would not be easily comprehended by Bangladesh.

Selective patronage was given to a small section of religious leadership, and the more 'fundamentalist' section became increasingly active politically. Government initiative triggered politicization of religious professionals a whole. In spite of the apparent distance from the fundamentalists, the government became vulnerable to their pressure. The net result of the government initiative for 'Islamisation'—increased social and political pressure against the minorities: the Hindus, the Christians, the Buddhists and the tribal who together constituted nearly 12 per cent of the national population. These minorities had to bear the brunt of Islamic pressure. A large section of the minority community tried to cross the border and enter

India from Bangladesh. They give a true story of misery and persecution at the socio-economic level. While minorities as a modern category of government and administration emerged in south Asia with the evolution of census, and the practice of enumerating diverse sections of population groups in the second half of the 19th century, minority politics acquires its importance insofar as they become an object of active discrimination. As the countries of south Asia grew into independent and sovereign states—thanks to decolonization and subsequent partition of the region—ethnic and communal minorities became an inseparable part of their existence.

Kabir Chowdhury in his book, *Maulabad Tar Itihash o Prakriti Anushandhan* gives excerpts from the speeches of Ershad on different occasions. He has been quoted in *Daily Ittefaq* as commenting that Islam should be at the topmost level of all religions. He further announced that Bangladesh was a country of Muslims and that their present struggle was to convert the country into an Islamic country. Moreover, he stressed on his fundamentalist stand by expressing the view, that by drawing the 'alpana' in Shahid Minar was anti-Islamic activity. In another peech delivered at the army camp on 13 November 1985, it becomes clear that Ershad was using religion to gain advantage in politics. He accused the Awami League government of eliminating the word 'Muslim' from the Salimullah Muslim Hall and claimed that he had restored Islam in the country by declaring Friday as weekly holiday.

When Islam was declared as the state religion on 6 June 1998, Bangladesh reached the level of a theocratic state, and the large population of Bangladeshis belonging to other religion like Hindus, Christians and Buddhists, were relegated into second class citizens in their own homeland. In order to demonstrate his love for Islam, Ershad's government granted some privileges to *madrasa* teachers, so that, in rural areas, madrasas began to eulogise Ershad. Anti-liberal ideas were preached inside mosques as well as at religious gatherings, such as *Waz* or *Mehfil*.

This journey of Bangladesh towards fundamentalism was conducted in a well-planned manner. Ziaur Rehman, Ershad and Khaleda Zia belonged to this category, and were joined by Golam Azam, Matiur Rehman Nizami and others who had formed and organized the fundamentalist, anti-liberal political party *Jamaat-e-Islami* and many other militant organizations. General Ershad had reasons to use religion in statecraft. In the first place, he wanted to convince the Muslims forming a homogenous majority in Bangladesh that he was dedicated to Islam. By appeasing the die-hard Muslims, he could cover up his licentious conduct in daily life. Secondly, and what is more important, Ershad intended to receive massive donations from the oil-rich Muslim countries for which an attitude of commitment to Islam might help.

Further, it was declared on many occasions that the assertion of political leadership by women was un-Islamic. The significance of such declarations became obvious when one noted that two ladies—Khaleda Zia and Sheikh Hasina—led the agitation against Ershad. Many women freedom fighters were intellectuals, like Shahid Janani Begum Jahanara Emam, Begum Sufia Kamal or Professor Akhtar Emam. In Pakistan, too, the late Benazir Bhutto sometimes faced a similar attack from religious fundamentalists.

The Ershad government was prepared to take steps calculated to appease the religious fundamentalists. During the eight and a half years of the rule of General Ershad, the influence of a religious leader from Atarshir increased so much that he interfered in many important matters of the state. The *Dargah* of this *Pir* was the place for economic transaction between the generals of the armies, well-placed bureaucrats and businessmen. Many other *Pir* s that arrived at this time, propagated about their supernatural powers by giving advertisement in the papers. The educated and well off persons also started visiting the *Dargah* of these *Pir*s. Although the treachery of these *Pir*s was reported in some newspapers, the hopelessness and economic deterioration in social life forced people to believe in luck. With a high rate of population growth, maldistribution of resources, hunger and natural disasters, Bangladesh became one of the poorest countries of the world. According to the United Nations Statistics, Bangladesh was one of the 36 Least Developed Countries. Predominantly rural, the average farm size in Bangladesh was 1.6 acres per household. Political string pulling and poverty was slowly pushing the country into the grip of conservatism.

In April 1990, at a public meeting in Bangabandhu Avenue, the Awami League announced that the establishment of a representative government, accountable to the people, was the only way out of the current crisis in the country, hoping that this would also be a measure against the spread of fundamentalism in the country. General Ershad soon found that he was losing control over the civil administration. Government employees marched out of the Secretariat on 3 December, 1990. At last, on 4 December, General Ershad tendered his resignation, and began to reside in the cantonment.

Ziaur Rehman had initiated the process of granting a high political status to forces opposed to the struggle for independence, and Ershad had consolidated them. That was why the military leaders, who ought to have been hanged as war criminals becaue of their role in the freedom movement of 1971, occupied important offices between 1975 and 1990. Military rulers were shrewd enough to remember that a large number of ordinary people had taken active part in the freedom struggle of 1971 and they used to swear in public. They repeatedly said that but for the participation of armed forces, the freedom struggle would have failed. The military element tried to impress upon the civil society that the armed forces were the superior elements in the society. Shrewdly enough they strengthened reactionary political parties who opposed the independence struggle of 1971, i.e., *Jamaat-e-Islami*.

A large section of minority community from Bangladesh find it alluring to come over to West Bengal and migrate here, perhaps because they do not enjoy such right in East Bengal, where property rights of the minority communities are not assured.[11] One reason for migration to West Bengal is the lack of security of the holdings of Hindu women. Extensive enquiries have been made as to the real position of property rights of women of minority communities, such as, the Hindus or the Buddhists. As yet, there has not been much movement for devolving a good and acceptable system of property rights of Hindu and Muslim women in Bangladesh and modern concepts of inheritance are not in vogue in Bangladesh. Hence, movements for property rights can be a part of the civil rights movement. The danger-point would be thrust on Bangladeshi refugees who would surely make the fears of the local Assamese of being swamped by outsiders.

In the nineties Bangladesh was accused of hosting the Inter-Service Intelligence of Pakistan that has fomented secessionist and terrorist activities in the north-east. The final denouements came when the Far Eastern Economic Review described Bangladesh as being a hotbed of militant Islam and India's Foreign Minister, Yashwant Sinha accused it of hosting Al Qaeda activists. Clearly Bangladesh has come a long way.

Aim of all political parties is to retain power and exploit the poor. As in many countries in the South, politics has become detached from ideology (one of the further consequences of the collapse of the Soviet Union). The rich Bangladeshis and politicians are not contemplating renunciation of their bank accounts abroad, nor of the education of their children in Australia or the USA.

On the other side, the defenders of the Bengali tradition want to see religion subordinated to an inclusive Bengali identity. They invoke great literary figures—national poet Nazrul Islam, Rabindranath Tagore—social reformers such as Begum Rokeya, pioneers of women's education such as Sufia Kemal, and fighters in two liberation struggles, against the British and the Pakistanis. They are threatened from many sides, by fundamentalism, western economic dominance with its business and pop culture, and by the power politics of India and the impact of Hindi movies upon the young.

The first of two cyclones that devastated Orissa in India late in 1999 sent its storms over southern Bangladesh. Jeremy Seabrook spent in Barishal a week as a time of incessant rain. The earth liquefied, ponds overflowed, lakes and pools drowned the land. The pale purple spindles of water hyacinths were coming into flower. These plants were brought to Bengal from the Mediterranean on a whim by Lady Hamilton. Within a decade they had colonized Bengal, choking the waterways, killing fish.

Without organization, some people would always struggle against disadvantage and oppression. The NGOs serve as focus for collective action. They simply make them more confident in their work for social and economic advancement. Much later, Seabrook spoke about his memories with Harun, Commander of British Brahmanbaria during the Liberation War.

Resisting the modern feudal mentality and its alliance with contemporary fundamentalism is central in the work of Proshikan, an NGO. This sometimes comes to open conflict. The foremost challenge came in brahmanbaria, where fundamentalists declared '*fatwa*' against Faruque, and threatened to kill him anywhere in Bangladesh.[12] His family were originally zamindars, but the system was reformed after partition, and his father's land had gone. Memories of feudal culture lingered into his childhood and Faruque struggled to reject all that.

He wanted to understand why some societies were dynamic, capable of change, while others remained static. In Europe, at the time of Renaissance, many people questioned everything, rejected ideas of religion and feudal society. Progress is made by logic, humanistic philosophy, and scientific development and so on.

Here a note may be added on the '*Baul*'s of East Bengal. The Bauls were a religious sect, a fusion of Muslim and Hindu belief, and their culture was characterized by mystic songs which, although devotional, are also sensuous, a celebration of nature and life. Tagore was influenced by Baul songs, and the Bangladesh national anthem is based on a Baul melody he heard. The Bauls are rooted in the south-west, around the present India-Bangladesh border.

Notes

1. Sukumar Biswas, Hiroshi Sato, *Religion and Politics in Bangladesh and West Bengal A Study of Communal Relations*, Joint Research Programme Series No. 99, Institute of Development Economies p. 55.
2. *Ibid.*, p. v.
3. *Ibid.*, p. v.
4. *Ibid.*, p. 86.
5. *Ibid.*, p. 146.
6. *Ibid.*, p. 146.
7. *Ibid.*, p. 150.
8. Ranabir Samaddar, *On Problems of Writing A Comprehensive History of the Bangladesh Liberation War*, p. 10 (Azad Institute Paper 6).
9. *Ibid.*, p. 10.
10. Jeremy Seabrook, *Freedom Unfinished.*
11. Dipankar Sengupta, Sudhir Kumar Singh, *Minorities and Human Rights in Bangladesh.*
12. Seabrook, p. 98.

9

Minority Sects in Bangladesh

A profile of Bangladesh as a country points out that by 1991 census, the religion-based division of the country is that: Islam (88.3%), Hinduism (10.5%), Buddhism (0.6%) and Christianity (0.3%). In a paper presented by Jose Kalapura S.J., there is a narration of Jesuit Hosten's sources for history of Churches in Asia[1] Hosten's interest in Church history was not limited by geographical boundaries. In his 'Collected Works', besides the details of the Christian Missions in the Mughal Empire (which included Dhaka and Pakistan), Jose Kalapura S.J. found references to sources on the Churches in Tibet (20), Burma (11), Nepal (8) and Cochin-China (4) etc.[2]

Within the Indian peninsula itself Kalapura SJ, obtained several references to Churches in Bengal (28), Pata and Bettiah (35) etc. These apart, there were articles on the works of other Religious Orders, points out Kalapura.[3] J. Felix Raj, SJ, further points out that, it was the conduct of the first two Jesuits in Bengal in 1576 that drew the attention of emperor Akbar to the Christian faith. When the two left, Fr. Gil Eanes Pereira of the Diocese of Cochin followed their mission in Bengal.[4] Jesuit priests returned to Bengal in 1598-9, with the intention of working there on a more permanent basis.

It was at Chandecan (Jessore) that the first Jesuit Church in Bengal was opened in January 1600. From Chandecan they proceeded to Sripur where Raja Kedar Rai was friendly. They also went to the great port of Chittagong and Dianga. Felix Raj, SJ, further points out that, from 1602 to 1615 the relations between the Portuguese and the King of Arakan (in whose territory these two places belonged) were generally hostile. The Jesuit Fathers were therefore imprisoned and the Christians were ill-treated. Kedar Rai of Sripur and the Raja of

Chandecan also did the same. Under these circumstances the surviving Jesuits left Bengal, some going to Pegu (Burma) and others returning to Cochin.

According to Kamruddin Ahmed, East Bengal had a dynamic middle class, which was determined to make East Bengal a modern society by breaking the hold of its traditionalist "mullah's and "peer's, its corrupt, intriguing and demagogic politicians, and the exploiters of the natural resources and industries. He also makes a further distinction between East and West Pakistan: he states that, while of all the non-Hindu countries in the world, East Bengal had the highest Hindu population and of all non-Buddhist countries, it had the highest Buddhist population, there was scarcely any religious minority in West Pakistan. This is certainly a unique and interesting view of East Bengal demography.

Three decades later, according to Dipankar Sengupta and Sudhir Kumar Singh, a sea-change is witnessed whereby Fundamentalists who had opposed the very creation of Bangladesh itself are now part of the ruling coalition of what is presently an Islamic Republic (i.e., Islam is the religion of the state).[5]

The Association for Diplomatic Studies and Training (ADST) research center twice welcomed retired ambassador and career diplomat Dennis Kux as a research fellow working on U.S.-Pakistan relations. In the year 1995, the ADST, together with Diplomatic and Consular Officers, Retired (DACOR), created the ADST-DACOR diplomats and Diplomacy Series to increase public knowledge and appreciation of the involvement of American diplomats in world history. The series seeks to demystify diplomacy by telling the story of those who had conducted their foreign relations, as they saw them, lived and reported them. *The United States and Pakistan, 1947-2000, Disenchanted Allies*, the result of Ambassador Kux's extensive research, was enthusiastically adopted for inclusion in this series.

The willingness of the retired Pakistani officials to share remembrances of their dealings with the United States had proven invaluable in helping him describe the rationale for Pakistan's actions and its perception of United States policies. In a series of articles published in the 'New York Times', American correspondents described the holocaust in Pakistan in 1971and its aftermath, and the reaction in the American strategic world.

President Bill Clinton's March 25, 2000, stop in Pakistan was once more ruled by the army of bilateral issues. How Pakistan dealt with the Taliban and other Islamic fundamentalists, and handled its tension-laden relations with India, vastly more dangerous since the two neighbours tested their nuclear weapons capabilities in May 1998, would have a decisive impact on United States interests in the subcontinent and beyond. Many disturbances took place in 1998, and when the fundamentalists started trouble, the work of the NGOs was halted, field workers were harassed, especially women.

There has been some bilateral support from European countries either through the government agencies or NGOs, especially in poverty alleviation programmes. International NGOs have also extended some support. A number of Muslim countries have provided assistance in establishing hospitals and educational institutions in Dhaka and beyond.[6] The burcaucrats who monopolized foreign credit also recognized that significant donor resources were going to NGOs.

Bangladesh as a member-state of the OIC (Organisation of Islamic Countries), have received support from the oil-rich countries of Saudi Arabia. Sheikh Hasina's Awami League government received support from the petro-dollar countries of the Arab World, and the country is economically dependent on the United States for all kinds of trade and investments. It has very little indigenous manufacture and most of the goods in the market flow from foreign countries of south-east Asia, such as Korea or Japan.

Bangladesh is not a country that invests on militarization, but much of the compilation of armaments has been done by Pakistan, and India, the big-brother. The SAARC countries do not always stress much on the policy of accumulation of nuclear equipments. Bangladesh is rather sandwiched between the giant military powers, compared to it, and it also shares a common border with Bhutan and China, which plays a significant role in the foreign relations of the country. A visit to the country shows that much of the development of roads and bridges has been done with the help of IMF and World Bank, and thereby the country has been overshadowed by foreign loans. But as according to Ranabir Samaddar and other researchers, the development of indigenous waterways has not been possible and the prospect of naval trade and transport through the Jamuna-Brahmaputra-Buriganga rivers, have come to a halt. Bangladesh is basically still a country of rickshaw-pullers, and the recent Nobel Prize won by Mohammed Yunus points out that, the Bangladeshis, every unit in the villages, are keen on agricultural banking.

According to K. Warikoo, 'Himalayan and Central Asian Studies Vol. 7 Nos. 3-4, July-Dec. 2003', Indian official trade with Bangladesh is over 1billion US dollars, with Indian exports over 900 million U.S. dollars. Therefore, the existing imbalance in bilateral trade can be set right if Bangladesh accepts the Indian offer of Free Trade Agreement (FTA).

With its proven natural gas reserves of about 23 trillion cubic feet (cft) and potential reserves of 60 trillion cft, Bangladesh can utilize its huge economic potential. As most of the gas fields are located in the north and eastern part of Bangladesh in close proximity to India, the export of surplus gas to India makes the best economic sense. Besides, India and Bangladesh can mutually benefit from collaborative ventures in exploration, transportation, industrial and commercial usage of natural gas. The sharing of water of the Ganges-Brahmaputra river over Farakka barrage in north Bengal, has given rise to various kinds of loss and economic bargains from both the countries.

As regards the transit facility to India's northeastern states through Bangladesh, it was in operation before the independence of Bangladesh. Though this matter was agreed upon Bangladesh and even included in the bilateral trade agreement signed in March 1972 and later in 1980, land transit facility has been denied to India. BIMSTEC (Bangladesh-India-Myanmar-Sri Lanka-Thailand-Economic Cooperation) offers an opportunity to both India and Bangladesh to collaborate in various sectors including transport, tourism, investment etc.

The Amnesty International has voiced its deep concern over the fate of religious minority groups in Bangladesh where collusion between politicians and criminals institutionalized the fundamentalist violence and corruption. This report pointed out that the Hindu minorities, the Buddhists tribesmen in Chittagong Hill Tracks and the Ahmedia Muslims—a moderate Islamic religious group—were made targets of attacks by fundamentalist ultras and diehard Islamic forces. The Amnesty International again has reasons to worry as the Dhaka administration was quite reluctant to hold any inquiry into the 2003 massacre of minority Buddhist tribes' men in Chittagong Hills.

"...The government had arrested thousands of Awami League workers in the wake of an opposition call for a nationwide *bundh* in April last year. They are still in detention without trial", the report said. Several human rights units and organisations of Bangladesh filed a petition jointly before High Court in September last year questioning propriety of such detention without trial.

The international rights body has vehemently criticized the Bangladesh administrations' "miserable failure" in tackling the situation. Nexus between a section of ruling politicians and fundamentalist ultras has made things worse, the report added. Different leaders, workers and organizers of democratic movement, opposition political leaders and activists are becoming victims of terrorist attack with human rights activists facing onslaught at various levels.

Notes

1. Goethals Seminar on 'Christian Contributions to Bengal', St. Xavier's College, Kolkata, Jan 22-23, 2006: 'Jesuit Hosten's Contributions to Bengal'.
2. *Ibid.*, p. 7.
3. *Ibid.*, p. 7.
4. St. Xavier's College, Kolkata.
5. Dipankar Sengupta, Sudhir Kumar Singh, *Minorities and Human Rights in Bangladesh*, p. xiii.
6. Nazrul Islam, *Dhaka Now*.

10

March Towards Islamization 1991-2004

The process which Ziaur Rehman had started was completed by Ershad. In this respect Ershad's most spectacular achievement was to declare Islam as the state religion of Bangladesh. As noted in the earlier chapters, the Islamization policy of Zia and Ershad resulted in splitting the nation on religious lines, whereas the nation had been united during the 1971 war of liberation on the basis of secular nationalism. Needless to say this division of the nation had served the interest of the military rulers.

Meanwhile, democratic process was gaining momentum in Bangladesh. The BNP and the pro-Zia faction of the army were already disgruntled. The Awami League which had by now greatly strengthened its position was also getting ready for a showdown. The massive movement of the combined opposition parties eventually led to the downfall of the Ershad regime in 1990.

After Ershad's downfall, the three alliances built up by the political groups, formed a caretaker government by placing the Chief Justice of High Court Sahabuddin Ahmed as President. For the first time in the history of Bangladesh, an election was held that did not have government interference. The main fundamentalist organization, the *Jamaat-e-Islami* secured only 18 seats amongst the 300 seats in the National Assembly.

Communal tension increased following the broadcast by the American Cable News Network through the State Run Bangladesh Television of the demolition of the Babri Masjid structure in India's Ayodhya town, on 6 December, 1992. The *Jamaat* and the *Islami*

Shashantantric Andolon (Islamic Constitutional Movement) activists while protesting against the incident, attacked Hindu temples and property. Between December 7 and 11 1992 such atrocities were reported from different parts of Bangladesh where 80 per cent of the 10 million people were Muslims.

A visit to the Ramakrishna Mission, Dhaka, and an interview with the *Swamiji*'s would reveal that the mission was the target of the fundamentalist Muslims many times, especially during the communal riots of 1992. Many Hindu structures were demolished; the *Sannyasis* had to look for shelters, and were afraid to speak frankly. One of the oldest Hindu religious institutions in Bangladesh, the Ramkrishna Mission suffered many times due to communal attacks, starting from 1905 or 1947 and 1971.

Another victim of the Muslims was the Hindu women of the rural areas or the Dhaka metropolis. They are extremely poor, and they have been the victims of rape, sexual abuse and many kinds of torture in the hands of the Pakistani army generals. Their stories have been written by many historians, such as Shariyar Kabir or Sukumar Biswas, and they are dispersed in different districts of Bangladesh, upto the frontier areas of the Chittagong Hill Tracts.

Anisuzzaman in his book, *Fatwa* (*1991-1995*), says that '*fatwa*'s were issued frequently in Bangladesh from 1991. He describes the communal activity of the *Mullahs* that was always prevalent in the rural areas of Bangladesh. A retired professor of Bengali from Dhaka University, Anisuzzaman was always aware of the terrorists who try to disturb the peace of the intelligentsia.

Anisuzzaman defines '*Fatwa*' to be the legal opinion regarding Islam as a religion. According to Anisuzzaman, Professor Syed Anwar Hossain and other leftist writers, '*Fatwa*' means relating to Islamic religion or religious opinions of Islamic people regarding revenue (*dewani)* transactions. Those who issue the '*Fatwa*'s are called '*mufti*'—people who possess tremendous knowledge or religious texts. Those who are consultants in this matter are called '*muftai*', they are real wise people in matters of theology. However, religious dictum on several matters comes from very old times, have been known to be used by the theologians. This kind of system is established not only in Islam but by the Christians as well. On several matters, they announced their extra-legal dictum under a legal garb, and had to be accepted by the people. Here we are going to look back to the past of Islamic history, and try to elucidate certain matters which came down to present times, even after Ershad's fall. First thing is '*Fatwa*', second, '*Mufti*'. Though these things originated a long time back, their nature may be discussed in the present context.

The '*muftai's* gave judgments as well, but generally their responsibility was confined to legal issues—the responsibility of judgment rested on the '*Quazi*'. Gradually, it fell upon the '*muftai*' to solve Islamic questions. The highest post was created fifty years ago—its name was Shaykhul Islam and was found to be existent and powerful at this time. But that post was terminated by Turkey, after the abolition of '*Khilafat*'. But at present, '*Fatwa*' committees were appointed by the state. Illustrations are Indonesia, Jordan, Turkey, Pakistan, Morocco, Malyasia., Egypt, Saudi Arab, Arabia and Sudan. Previously, the Al-Azhar University at Egypt or the 'Deoband' school issued '*Fatwa*', who did not interfere in criminal justice, and did not have any rights. The limitation was that, in colonial rule, 'Fatwa' was not accepted in totality, but by all sections of the people.

But in today's Bangladesh, even after the fall of Ershad, the issue of granting '*fatwa*'s took a big turn, and it has become an ordinary event. Anisuzzaman in his book, *Fatwa*, observes that, there are many illustrations of giving 'Fatwa' in Bangladesh. He points out that, many artisans and littérateurs-professors have been given capital punishment due to non-conformist and irreligious activities in the city under this coalition government. In the villages, physical punishment is given to the down-trodden people, especially women, by lodging complains of demoralization against them. One such instance is that in January 1993, the fundamentalists lodged a false complain against a young woman named Nur Jahan in the Sylhet district and gave her punishment—half of her body would be buried inside the earth and 101 stones would be thrown at her. This cruel punishment was implemented in front of all the rural people. When the news came to be known through the media, the progressive writers and the socialists vehemently protested. The suicide of the harassed woman, Nur Jahan, thus gave a big shake to the hearts of the people.

The news of Nur Jahan's death created a serious situation in the whole village. Her father Asrafullah cried and appealed to the Panchayet that the disaster has already taken place. Arrangements should be made for her burial. But the Maulana declined and said that it is not an easy task to bury that dead body. According to '*Banglabazar Patrika*', dated 15.1.93, in the night of 10th January Asrafullah went to Kamalgunge police station to report the whole tragedy.[1]

Investigation started on the issue of Noorjahan's death in Kamalgunge.[2] Pranab Saha and Akmal Hussain Nipu reported from Maulavigunge, that there was investigation on the event of death of Noorjahan Lakshmi started through unions in Chatakchara village. According to 'Bhorer Kagoj', there were a few witnesses including dead Noorjahan's father Asrafullh.[3] The police was yet to receive the postmortem report of dead Noor Jahan.

On the other hand, the *Jamaat-e-Islami* and such other organizations supported the action of cruelty on Noor Jahan by the fundamentalists. Shockingly enough, the government remained silent, and the local government in certain areas took minimum steps against the fundamentalists. Strangely enough, the main opposition party Awami League also remained silent like the BNP for the fear of losing votes of the fundamentalists. Noor Jahan was so cruelly treated because her sin was that she wanted to marry Motleb, a resident of the same village. So NoorJahan committed suicide by taking insecticides. A case was called up in the Kamalgunge police station.

In the meantime the central leadership of the Village council went to the Chatakchara village of Kamalgunge on 12 April. They laid floral tributes on the grave of Noor Jahan. Under the leadership of woman Vice-President Baby Moudud, central committee member Khaleda Mahbub and others talked to NoorJahan's father, mother and husband, and rendered sympathies on the tragic death of Noor Jahan.[4] This was a society which basically Bangladesh was, utterly superstitious and ignorant, and the burden of such a society now was taken up by present government.

According to *The Daily Star*, dated 28 January, 1993, the family, with its basic axis of the sexual division of labour, is its principal underlying institution.[5] The violence of beating or torturing women to death in privacy or even, as in this case, publicly, has to be examined and needs much attention to comprehend the social condition of Bangladesh. NoorJahan was charged of violating the Muslim law whereas in Quranic precepts, no such atrocities are prescribed by the original Islamic tenet. It is the *Fatwa*, the '*Mufti*' and the '*Quazi*', who were taking control of the society. Sigma Huda, the noted lawyer added, here the Imam and the Panchayet leaders are criminals. They do not have any right to take laws in their own hands, and adjust it according to their wish.

The death of NoorJahan has once again brought in view the desperate situation. According to '*Bhorer Kagoj*', dated 3 February, 1993, there was a legal battle regarding the incident at Kamalgunge. Reliable sources from Maulavibazar pointed out that, a definite legal case has begun against the accused, in Kamalgunge district regarding the death of helpless young housewife, Noor Jahan Lakshmi (aged 22).

It is noteworthy that on 10 January on the basis of '*Fatwa*', issued by the Imam, the second marriage of the young housewife Noor Jahan Lakshmi was declared illegal, and she was publicly persecuted by throwing stones at her. Noor Jahan could not endure this insult and committed suicide. The accused have been taken to trial by the legal suite 306/504/109.

Immediately after this barbarious incidence a three member team of Maleka Begum, Khaleda Mahoob and Baby Moudud, from Bangladesh Mahila Parishad went to Chatakchara village of Moulavibazar district in Sylhet. This organisation, which has been fighting to implement womens' right for years together, went to investigate the case.

The policy of appeasement of fundamentalists by the political parties gave moral courage to the *Jamaat* and on 29 December, 1991, they announced Azam's appointment as the *Amir*, sparking off immediate protest across Bangladesh. On 19 January, 1992, as a repercussion to this move, Bangladesh's 101 well-known personalities including retired Supreme Court judges, university teachers, veterans of the independence war, artists and journalists formed the "Committee to Uproot the Killers and Collaborators of the 1971 independence war." Thousands of people from all walks of life supported the move and to incorporate their representatives in the framework of the campaign, the "National Coordinating Committee for Realization of Bangladesh Liberation Ideals and Trial of Bangladesh War Criminals of 1971" was formed. The Coordinating Committee set-up the investigation of the action of collaborators on 26 March 1993. Its report that came one year later, announced the names of eight people, of which five belonged to the *Jamaat*. Its campaign, the largest and most powerful in the history of Bangladesh, also found support from expatriate Bangladeshis. A people's court chaired by Jahanara Imam announced death punishment for Golam Azam on the occasion of twenty-fifth Independence Day of Bangladesh. However, it could not be implemented.

The *Jamaat* was joined by rightwing Freedom Party and other fundamentalist groups to form the "Committee to resist Indian collaborators". Its objective was to create obstacles in the public functions of the National Coordinating Committee and its members. The government at the same time issued warrants and arrested some leading members of the Nirmul Committee and Coordinating Committee across Bangladesh.

It had been assumed that the Awami League would receive the majority vote and come to power in the elections of 1991, but in reality BNP came to govern. After the defeat in this election, the leadership of the Awami League understood the importance of the use of religion in politics. Therefore, during the elections of 1996, the Awami League attached importance to the criticism of opposition denouncing the Awami League as 'Indian agent'. As a reply to such ideas, the Awami League had to make anti-Indian speeches favouring Islam, which disappointed many supporters of the Awami League.

The Bangladesh National Party called an election on 15 February 1996 without the participation of the opposition. Jamaat-e-Islami's seats dwindled from 19 to 2. Before 1996, student fronts in Bangladesh were the main players in politics. But civil society is now the main participant, especially NGOs. This corresponds to a degradation of students influence on political movements, through the control of students by the parties.

Although Professor Golam Azam retired from the post of '*Amir*', still he participated in the politics of '*Jamaat-e-Islami*' as earlier. He took this decision because he wanted to create new leadership after the '96 elections. An interview of Professor Golam Azam would reveal that, the rise of fundamentalism in Bangladesh was interwined with the development of '*Jamaat-e-Islami*'. A group of fundamentalists were not satisfied with the *Jamaat*, considered it too soft and non-militant. But the truth was that, the *Jamaat* and the anti-*Jamaat* fundamentalists stood on one platform often when fundamentalism was really at trial. In the freedom struggle of 1971, all the fundamentalists and the communal organizations including the *Jamaat-e-Islami* stood behind the army rule of Pakistan to protect 'Islam in distress', and in the communal unrest of 1992, the Jamaat and the anti-Jamaat forces worked together. Adopting the styles of the Nazi and the fascist parties, the armed workers of the *Jamaat-e-Islami* did not hesitate to murder the workers of the competitive political parties.

Whereas the Islamic fundamentalist outfit *Shahadat-e-al-Hakima*, which advocates the occupation of West Bengal by Bangladesh, has been banned by Bangladesh in February 2003, it needs to initiate similar action against other organizations operating against India from Bangladeshi soil. Given Bangladesh's commitment to the global campaign against terrorism, it would be in Dhaka's interest to curb the rise of Islamic extremism and terrorism. Bangladesh should continue to be seen as a moderate, pluralistic society committed to regional peace, democratic values and practices.

"The Committee to Uproot the Killers and Collaborators of the Independence War" formed by Jahanara Imam started with a demand for the trial of war criminal Golam Azam. It accelerated the movement against communalism and fundamentalism, towards the realization of the spirit of the freedom movement. However, the political parties which supported the movement were more interested in the trial of war criminals, particularly Golam Azam. Even when the movement reached its climax, the political parties disliked the use of the word, 'fundamentalism'. The Nirmul Committee took a strong stand in this regard and the word "fundamentalism" was incorporated in all its slogans and posters.[6]

The Awami League came to office in 1996 and was also propagating against communalism and fundamentalism. To remove the Awami League from power, most of the communal parties have combined with BNP. The *Jamaat* which had previously considered BNP to be an evil party and woman leadership as *haram* (sin) is now the main supporter of BNP. They are spreading the sentiments of communalism by campaigning against *Shikha Chirantan* or the *Parbatya Chattagram* Peace Treaty and consequently the Awami League has to speak against communalism and fundamentalism. Simultaneously, the government has to implement other kinds of work schedules like the spread of *madrasa* education and to make religious educational system compulsory.

In the future when BNP next comes to power, then Blasphemy Law and Shariya Law might be implemented in Bangladesh as it had been done in Pakistan. The minority communities and religious minorities would be forced to leave the country and the whole nation might slip into the darkness of the Middle Ages.

In 1997, the Awami League government signed an accord with the leaders of the people of the Chittagong Hill Tracts. The grievances of the hill women, their demand for rights and autonomy, has been written and elaborated in several pamphlets. One such illustration may be a pamphlet named, 'Paharer Ruddhakantha', which deals with the women tribal leaders, like Kavita Chakma. The hill women are more stern and humourous than their Bengali counterpart. Their lost voices and search for identity has been written by scholars like Meghna Guhathakurta and Raja Devasish Roy, who was the chief of the Chakma, presented a precise description of the unique legal and administrative system that had no parallel in other parts of Bangladesh.[7]

Meghna Guhathakurta, a careful monitor of the CHT, tells the story of hill women's vulnerability and suffering, who contribute enormously to the building of their families and communities. The ethnic women, despite their contribution in building communities, are less fortunate in possessing property. They are defenseless against various kinds of human rights including rape.

The first article by Philip Gain gives an overview of the geography, people, land, economy, forest and human rights condition in the CHT. He describes how incidents throughout the past half-century have changed the CHT to such a great extent. In another essay, Proshanta Tripura makes his point that 'development' in the CHT has always meant dislocation and disruption of life and nature. It is time for the development agents to understand the dynamics of culture and identity of the CHT people. The government entered into many treaties with the CHT, and still the refugee question in this area remains unanswered. The *Shanti Bahini* has been unable to restore peace in the north-east.

Badruddin Umar has written a book, *Bangladesher Communist Andolone Shamoshya*, where he tries to analyse the rise and fall of leftist politics in Bangladesh, an untrodden ground. He discusses how he resigned from the East Pakistan Communist Party (Marxist-Leninist) in December 1971, due to much difference in opinion and principles in the warfront. From 1972, he started discussing the matter with different groups.

Notes

1. *Fatwa 1991-1995*, edited by Anisuzzaman and others.
2. *Ibid.*, p. 9.
3. *Ibid.*, p. 9.
4. *Fatwa*, p. 10.
5. *Fatwa*, p. 13.
6. Nirmul Committee, *Resist Fundamentalism: Focus on Bangladesh*, Dhaka, Dana Printers, 1999.
7. Philip Gain edited, *The Chittagong Hill Tracts Life and Nature at Risk.*

Select Bibliography

English

A.F. Salahuddin Ahmed, *India, Pakistan and Bangladesh Perspectives on History Society and Politics.*

A.K. Niazi, *The Betrayal of East Pakistan.*

Asim Roy, *Islam in South Asia.*

Ayesha Jalal, *The State of Martial Rule: The Origins of Pakistan's Political Economy of Defence*

——, *The Sole Spokesman Jinnah, the Muslim League and the Demand for Pakistan.*

Bipan Chandra, *Modern India* (National Council for Educational Research and Training).

——, A. Tripathi, Barun De, *Freedom Struggle.*

Chandi Prasad Sarkar, *The Bengali Muslims: A Study in their Politicization (1912-1919).*

Christopher Hill, *The Intellectual Origins of the English Revolution.*

Dennis Kux, *Estranged Democracies.*

Edward Said, *Orientalism.*

Encyclopedia on Religion.

General G.W. Chowdhury, *The Last Days of United Pakistan.*

Gita Roy, *The Duel of the Decade.*

Jayanta Kumar Ray, *Nationalism and Democracy on Trial* (1968).

Jeremy Seabrook, *Freedom Unfinished.*

Joya Chatterjee, *Bengal Divided: Hindu Communalism and Partition 1932-47.*

Jyoti Sengupta, *The Eclipse of East Pakistan Since Birth of Bangladesh till October 1963.*

Kathleen Gough and Hari P. Sharma, edited, *Imperialism and Revolution in South Asia.*

Mizanur Rehman Shelly, *Emergence of a new nation in a multi-polar world, Bangladesh* (1979).
Muhammad Nurul Qadir, *Independence of Bangladesh In 266 Days History and Documentary Evidence.*
Muntasir Mahmood, Jayanta Kumar Ray, *Civil Society in Bangladesh Resilience and Retreat.*
Mushirul Hassan, edited, *India's Partition Process, Strategy and Mobilization.*
Nazrul Islam, *Dhaka Now.*
Partha Chatterjee, *Bengal: The Land Questions.*
Philip Gain, edited, *The Chittagong Hill Tracts Life and Nature at Risk.*
Prafulla Kumar Chakrobarty, *The Marginal Men.*
Rafiuddin Ahmed, edited, *Religion, Nationalism and Politics in Bangladesh.*
Rounaq Jahan, *Pakistan: Failure in National Integration* (1972).
Salahuddin Ahmed, *India Pakistan Bangladesh Perspectives on History Society and Politics.*
Siddiq Saliq, *Witness to Surrender.*
Sreeradha Datta, *Bangladesh: A Fragile Democracy*, Shipra Publications, Delhi.
Sukumar Biswas, Hiroshi Sato, *Religion and Politics in West Bengal: A Study of Communal Relations.*
Tariq Ali, *Can Pakistan Survive? The Death of a State* (1972)
——, *Pakistan: Military Rule or People's Power.*
Tazeen M. Murshed, *The Sacred and the Secular Muslim Discourses 1871-1977.*
The Quran (translation).

Bengali

A.S.M. Abdul, Hi *Bhabishayate Islamic Shiksha.*
Abul Hashim, *Amaar Jiban o bibhagpurba Bangladesher Rajnity.*
Anisuzzaman, edited, *Fatwa* (1995)
——, *Amar Ekattor.*
Atiur Rehman and Lenin Azad, edited, *Bhasha Andolon Pariprekhit o Bichar,* volumes 1, 2.
Atiur Rehman and Syed Hashemi, *Angshogrohonkarider Sreni Abosthan,* volume 4.

Azizur Rehman Mallik, *Amar Jibankatha o Bangladesher Muktishangram.*

Badruddin Umar, *Purba Banglar Bhasha Andolon o Tatkalin Rajnity,* volumes 1, 2, 3

——, *Bangladeshe Communist Andoloner Shamashya*

——, *Ekattorer Swadhinata Juddher Pathe.*

Basanti Guhathakurta, *Kaler Bhalay.*

Golam Azam, *Chintadhara.*

Hasan Hafizur Rehman, edited, *Purba Banglar Swadhinata Shangrame Dalil o Dastabej,* volumes 1 to 12.

M.M. Akash, *Srenibhittik o Rajnoitik Prabonotashomuho,* volume 3.

Mohammed Kamruzzaman, *Islamic Ganatantric Rashtra Shamakalin Paristhite.*

Ratanlal Chakrobarty, *Bangladesher Dalil o Shangbadpatre Netaji Subhash.*

Shariyar Kabir, edited, *Ekattorer Dushaho Smriti.*

Sukumar Biswas, *Bangladesher Muktijuddhe CPIM o Ganashakti* (2001).

Newspapers, Journals and Pamphlets

Anisur Rehman, *The Lost Moments Dreams with a nation born through fire Papers on Political Economy of Bangladesh.*

Forum, April 25, 1970.

Mediar Mukhomukhi Golam Azam.

Morning News, Karachi Friday, January 22, 1960, Volume VII, No. 158 (Abanti Adhikari).

South Asian Review, volume 3, no. 3.

Sunday Morning News, January 17, 1960.

Index